RECORDED VERSIONS GUITAR

AUTHENTIC TRANSCRIPTIONS
WITH NOTES AND TABLATURE

Jeff Buckley

COLLECTION

Exclusive Distributors:
Music Sales Limited
8/9 Frith Street, London W1D 3JB, England
Music Sales Pty Limited
120 Rothschild Avenue, Rosebury, NSW 2018, Australia

Order No. AM976525
ISBN: 0-7119-9831-0

D1335867

Music transcriptions by Pete Billman
Cover photograph © S.I.N./Corbis

from *Grace*

Dream Brother

Words and Music by Jeff Buckley, Mick Grondahl and Matt Johnson

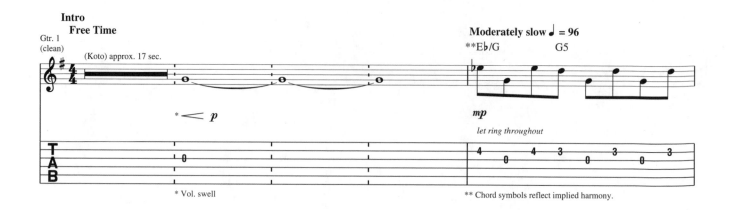

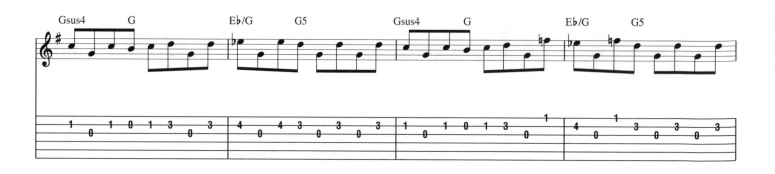

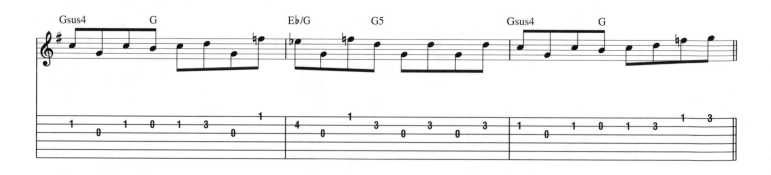

Verse

1. There is a child sleep-ing near his twin, _ the pic-tures go wild in a rush of wind. _

4

Gtr. 1: w/ Rhy. Fig. 1

wait - ing for you __ like I wait - ed for mine __ and   no - bod - y   ev - er __ came. __

Interlude

Gtr. 1

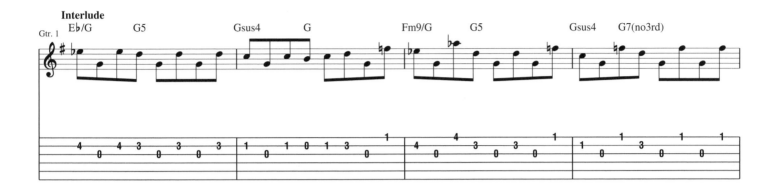

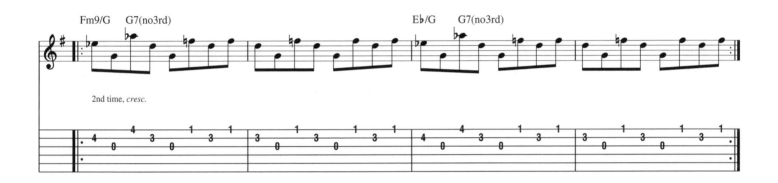

2nd time, *cresc.*

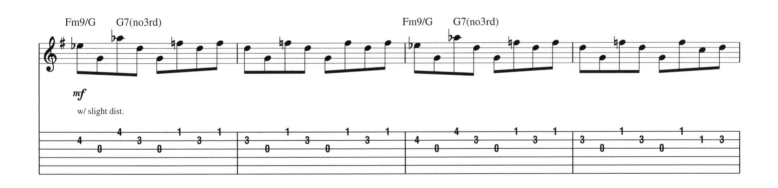

mf

w/ slight dist.

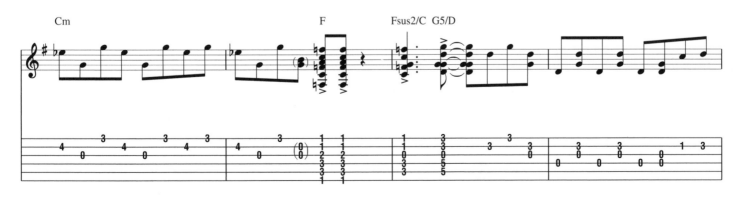

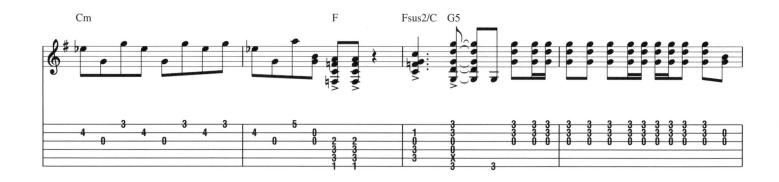

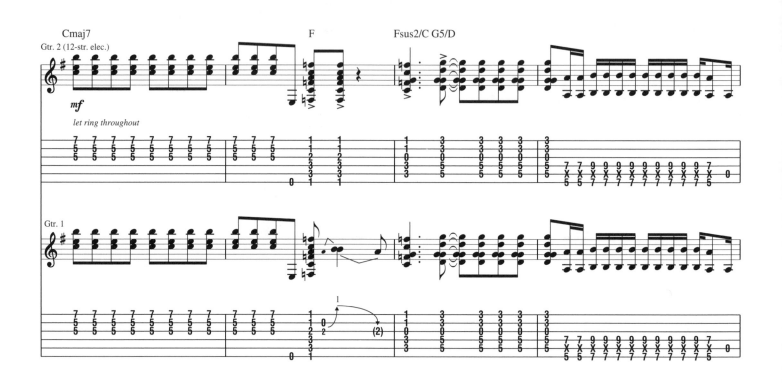

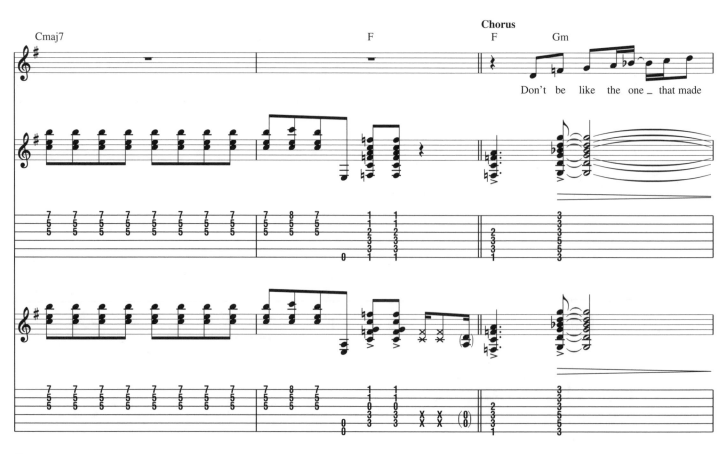

Don't be like the one _ that made

me so old. Don't be like the one you left be-hind his __ name 'cause they're

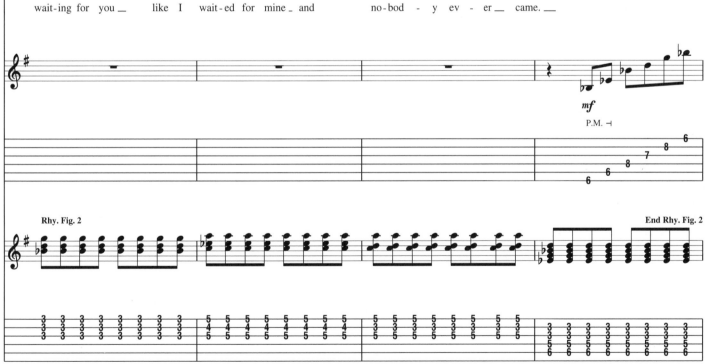

wait-ing for you __ like I wait-ed for mine __ and no-bod — y ev-er __ came. __

Rhy. Fig. 2

End Rhy. Fig. 2

Gtrs. 1 & 2: w/ Rhy. Fig. 2 (2 times)

Don't be like the one __ who made me so old. Don't be

like   the   one   who   left   be - hind   his _ name   'cause they're   wait - ing   for   you _   like   I

wait - ed   for   mine _   and   no - bod - y   ev - er _   came. _   (No - bod - y   ev - er _   came.) _

Interlude

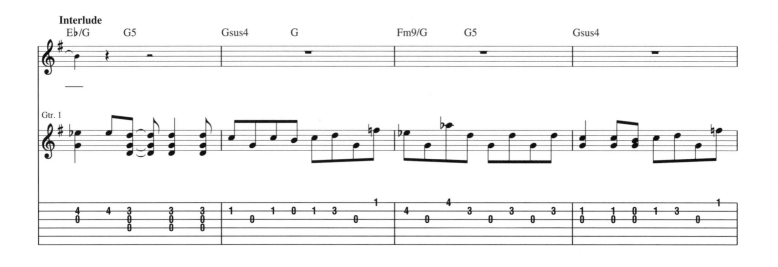

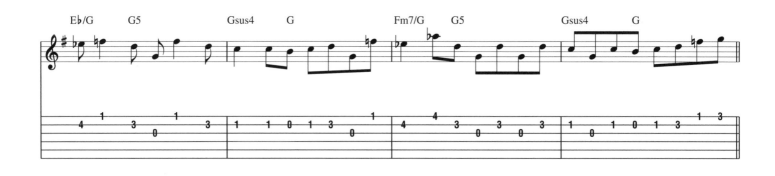

Verse

3. I feel a - fraid   and I   call your   name. _   I love your voice   and your dance in - sane. _   I

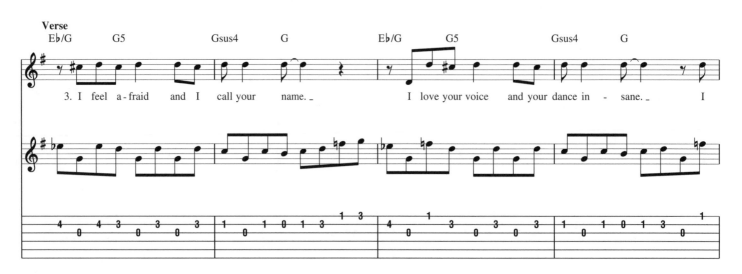

* Depress strings behind nut.

from *Grace*

Eternal Life

Words and Music by Jeff Buckley

Intro
Moderately ♩ = 96
N.C.(E5)
Gtr.1 (clean)

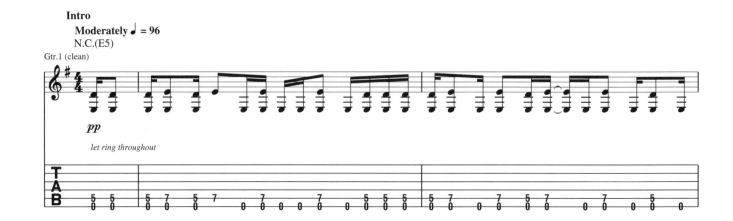

pp

let ring throughout

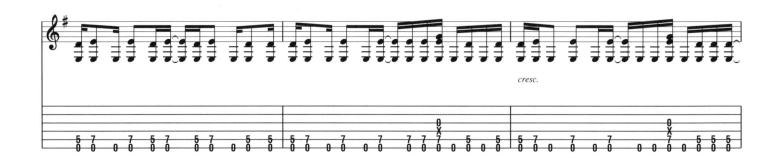

cresc.

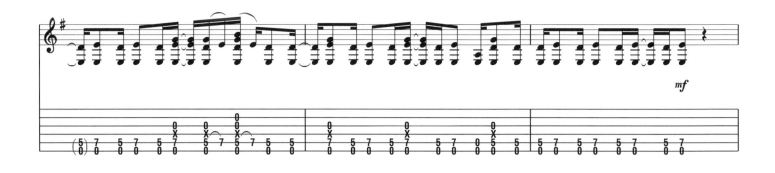

mf

E   Dadd4   E   D6add4

f w/ dist.

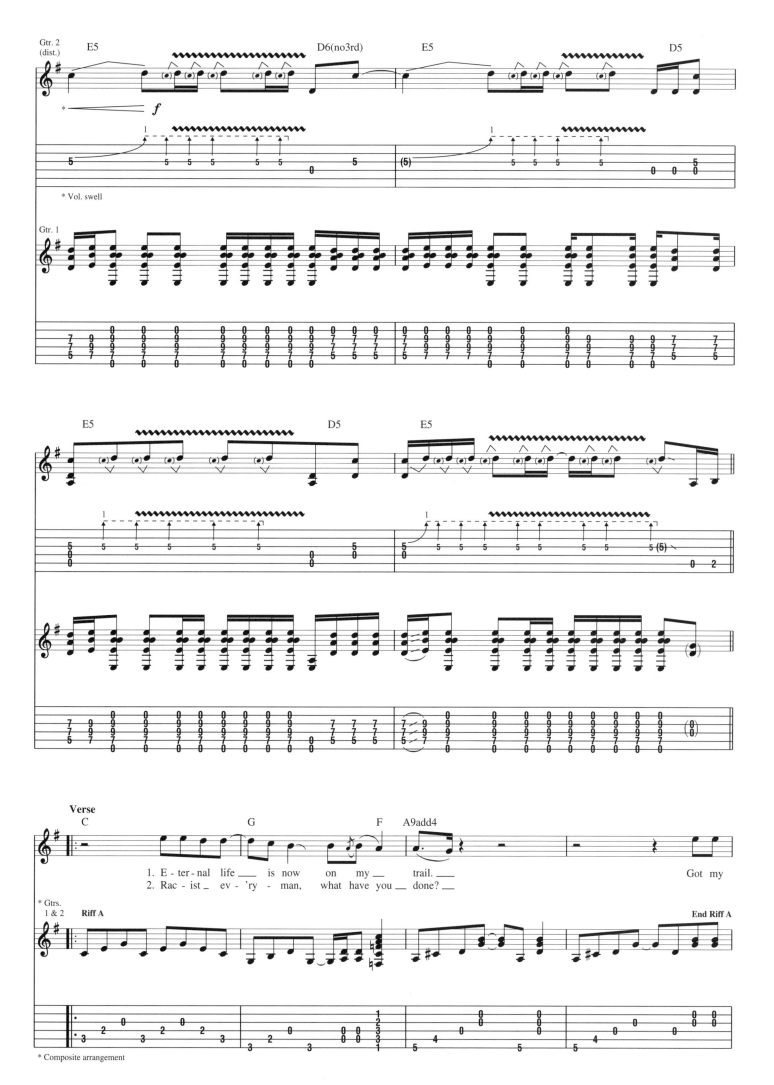

red glit-ter cof-fin, man. Just need a one last ___ nail.
Man, you've made a kill-er of your un - born

___ son. While all these ug-ly gen-tle-men ___
Oh, ___ crown my ___ fear ___ your

play out their fool-ish games, ___ there's a
king at the point of a gun. ___

flam-ing red ho-ri - zon that screams ___ our names. ___
All I wan-na do ___ is a love ___ ev-'ry-one. ___

Chorus

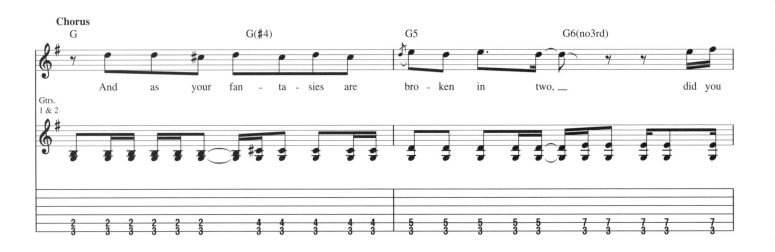

And as your fan-ta-sies are bro-ken in two, ___ did you

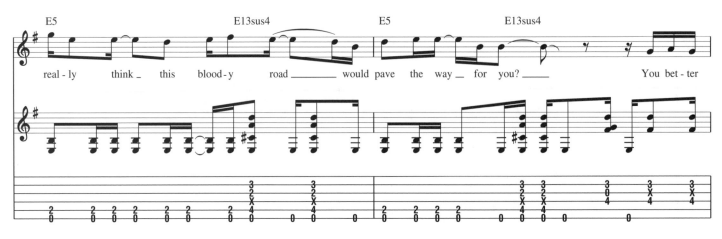

real-ly think ___ this blood-y road ___ would pave the way ___ for you? ___ You bet-ter

doh, _____ huh. _____

C#°   C   F#7   Fmaj7

There's no time for _____ ha - tred, on - ly ques - tions. What is love? _____

Gtr. 3 (clean)

Gtrs. 1 & 2

p

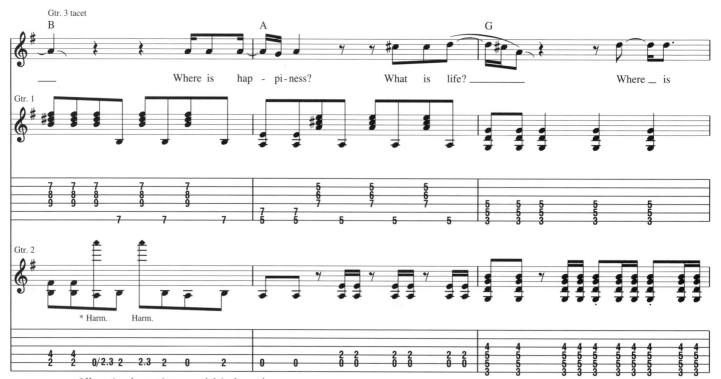

Gtr. 3 tacet

B   A   G

_____ Where is hap - pi - ness? What is life? _____ Where _ is

Gtr. 1

Gtr. 2

* Harm.   Harm.

* Harmonic and open string are sounded simultaneously.
  Harmonic located three-tenths the distance between 2nd & 3rd frets.

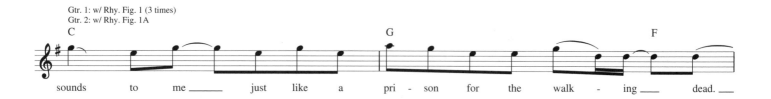

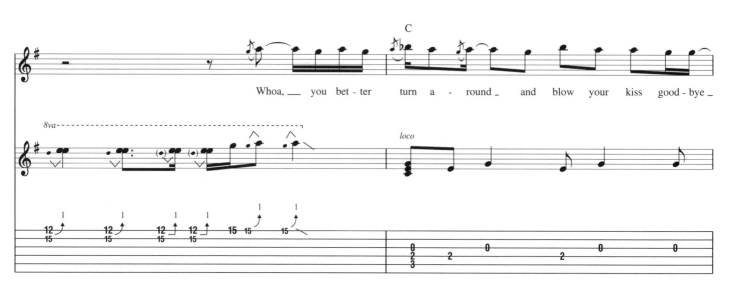

An - gel, _____ oo, _____ yeah, _____ yeah. _____

Uh!

* w/ misc. fdbk. & electronic noise.

from *Sketches for My Sweetheart the Drunk*—disc 1

Everybody Here Wants You

Words and Music by Jeff Buckley

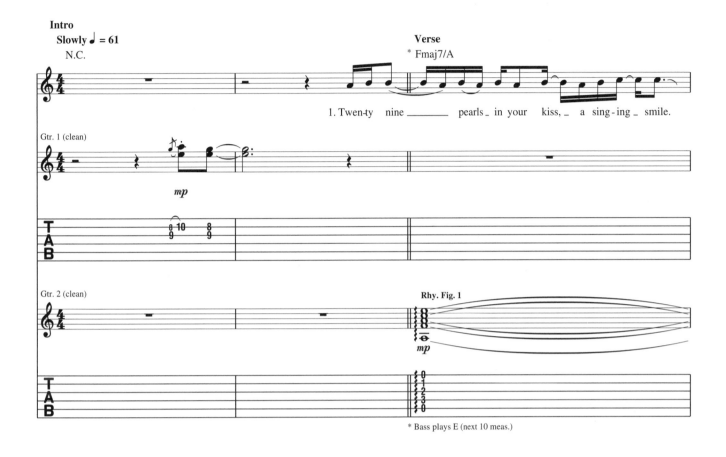

* Bass plays E (next 10 meas.)

pearls _ in your kiss, _ a sing-ing _ smile. Cof - fee _ smell and li - lac skin, _ your flame in _ me. _

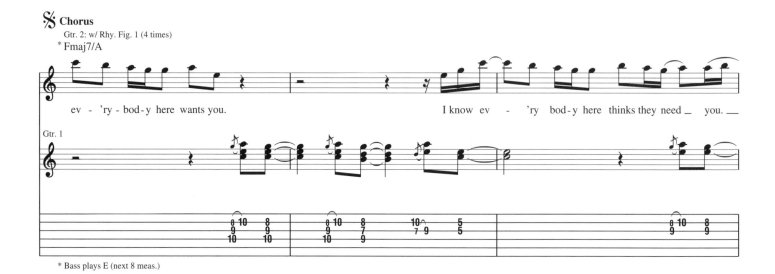

I'm _ on - ly here _____ for this _ mo - ment. _ I know

§ **Chorus**

Gtr. 2: w/ Rhy. Fig. 1 (4 times)
* Fmaj7/A

ev - 'ry-bod-y here wants you. I know ev - 'ry bod-y here thinks they need _ you. _

Gtr. 1

* Bass plays E (next 8 meas.)

To Coda ⊕

I'll be wait - in' right here just to show you how _ our _

Verse

Gtr. 2: w/ Rhy. Fig. 1 (5 times)
** Fmaj7/A

_ love _____ will blow it all a - way. _ 2. Mm, such a _ thing of won - der in this crowd.

** Bass plays E (next 10 meas.)

20

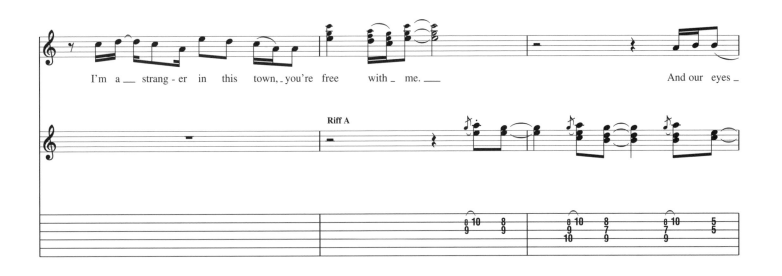

I'm a ___ strang-er in this town, ___ you're free with ___ me. ___ And our eyes ___

___ locked in out-cast love, ___ I sit here ___ proud. E - ven ___ now you're un-dressed in ___ your dreams with ___ me. ___

End Riff A

D.S. al Coda

Oh, ___ I'm on - ly here ___ for this ___ mo - ment. ___ I know

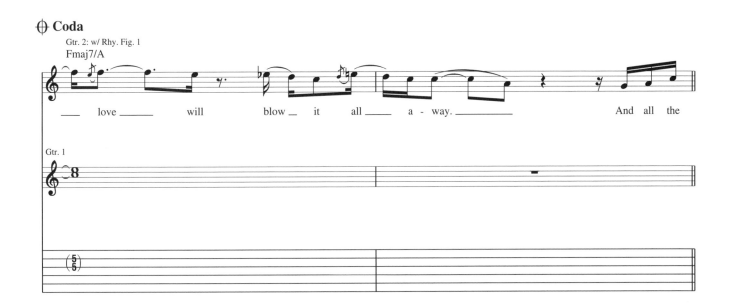

⊕ Coda

Gtr. 2: w/ Rhy. Fig. 1

Fmaj7/A

___ love ___ will blow ___ it all ___ a - way. ___ And all the

Gtr. 1

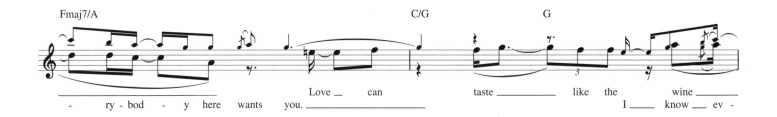

- ry-bod - y here wants you. _____ Love _ can taste _____ like the wine _____ I _ know ev -

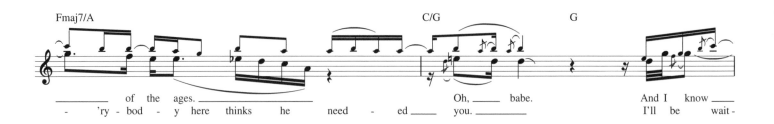

_____ of the ages. _____ Oh, _ babe. And I know _____
- 'ry-bod - y here thinks he need - ed _____ you. I'll be wait -

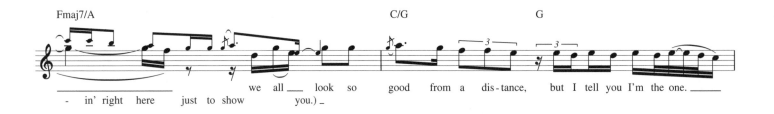

- in' right here just to show you.) _ we all _ look so good from a dis - tance, but I tell you I'm the one. _____

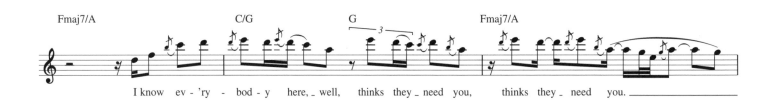

I know ev - 'ry - bod - y here, _ well, thinks they _ need you, thinks they _ need you. _____

Free time

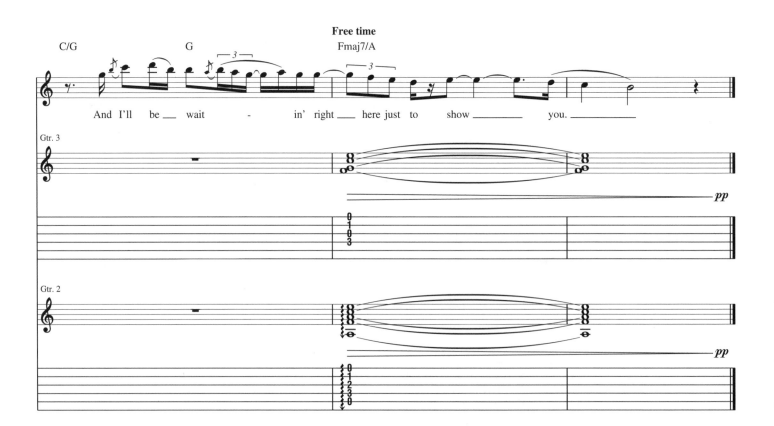

And I'll be _ wait - in' right _ here just to show _____ you. _____

Gtr. 3

Gtr. 2

Grace

Word and Music by Jeff Buckley and Gary Lucas

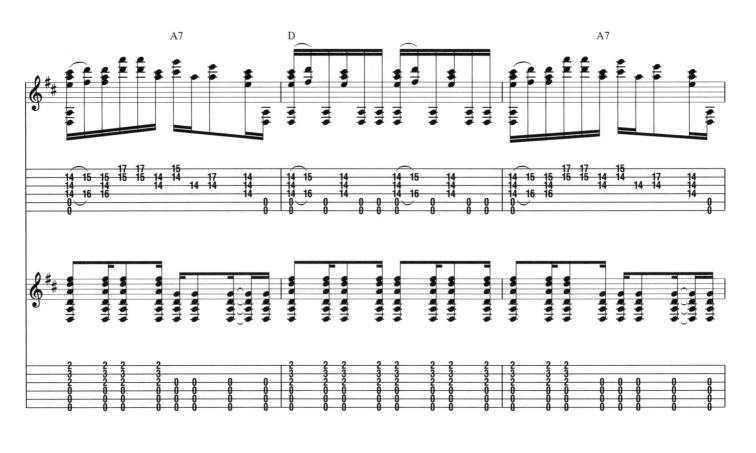

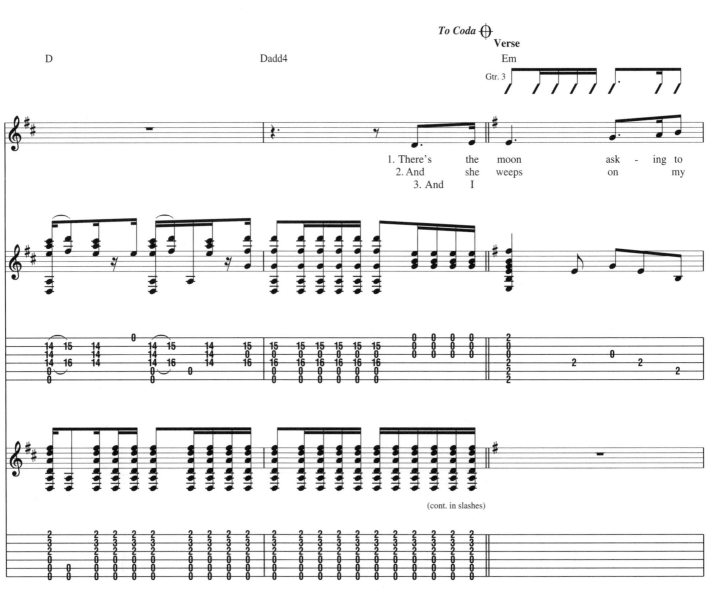

1. There's the moon ask - ing to
2. And she weeps on my
3. And I

(cont. in slashes)

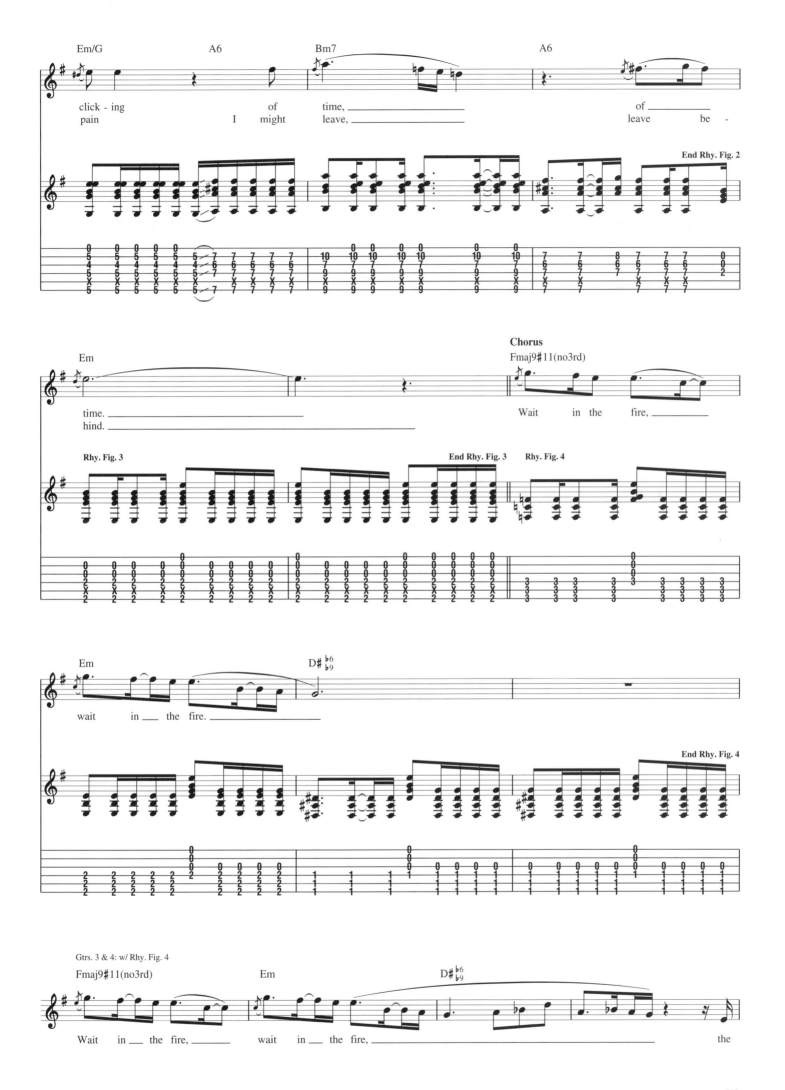

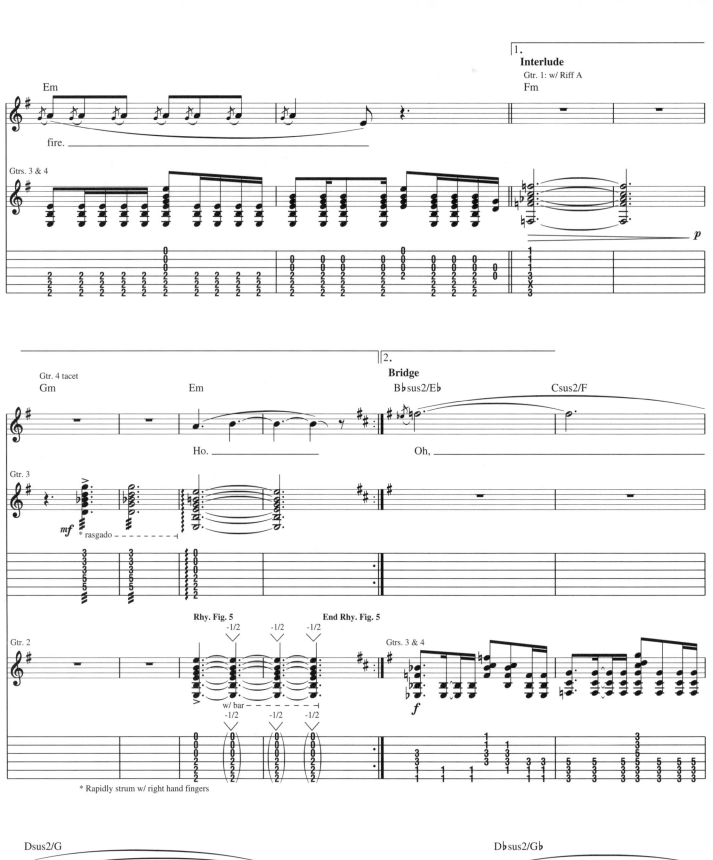

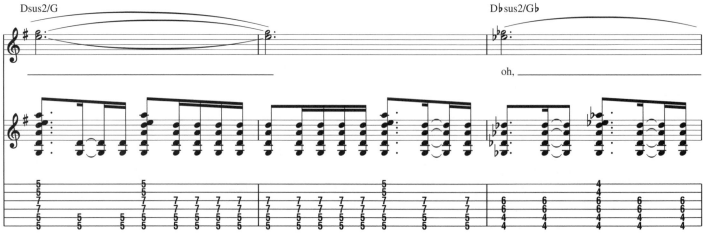

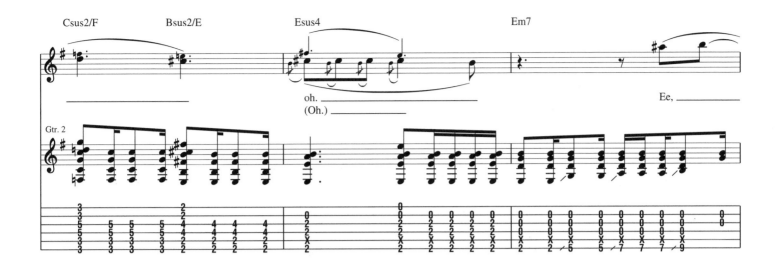

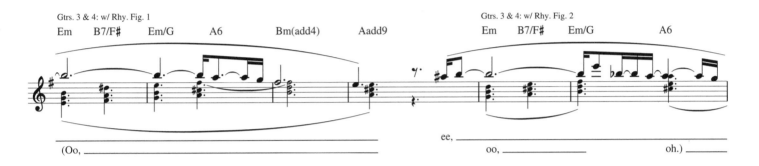

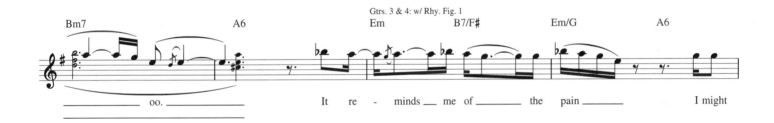

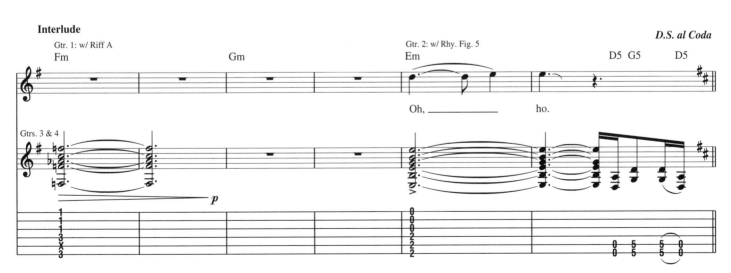

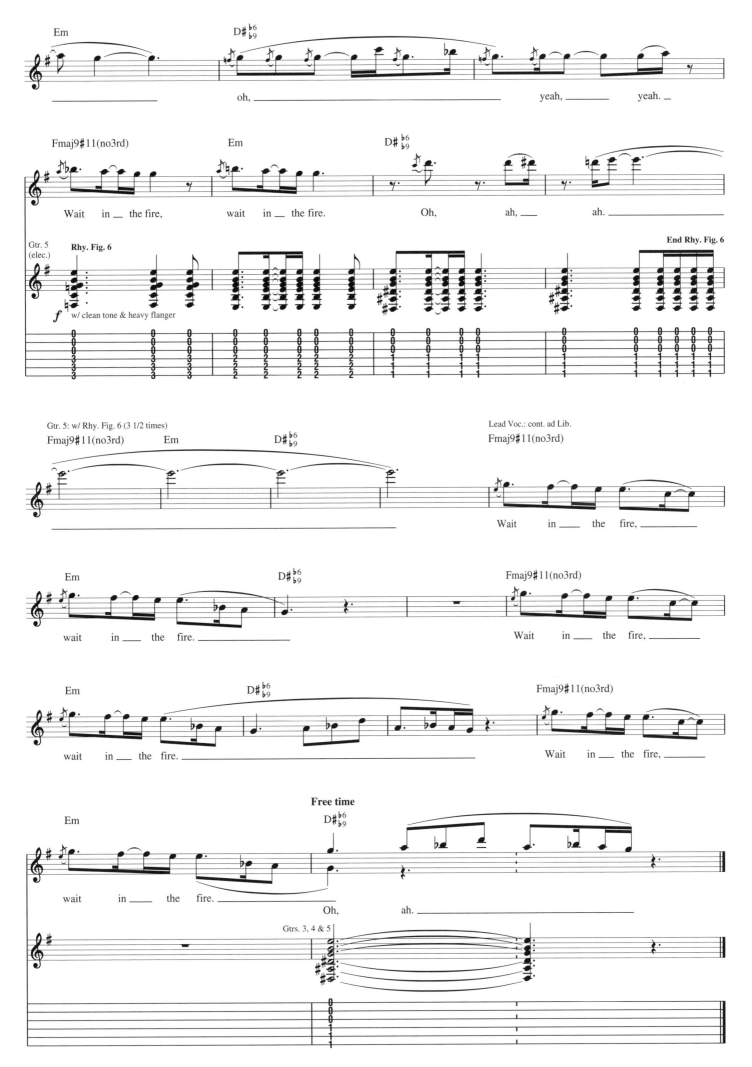

Haven't You Heard

Words and Music by Jeff Buckley

Verse

Gtr. 1: w/ Rhy. Fig. 1

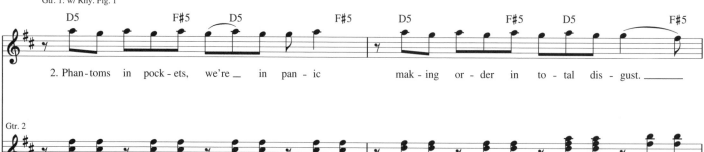

2. Phan - toms in pock - ets, we're __ in pan - ic mak - ing or - der in to - tal dis - gust. _____

Gtr. 2

Oh, they read a list of who can - not stay, take you down on the ground.

Chorus

Gtr. 1: w/ Rhy. Fig. 2
Gtr. 2: w/ Riff A (1 1/2 times)

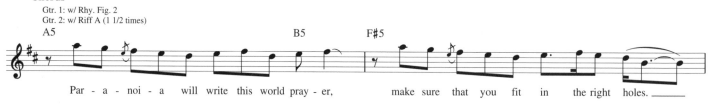

Par - a - noi - a will write this world pray - er, make sure that you fit in the right holes. _____

But when you take this of - fer you're done for, done for. Oh, _____

Oh. _____

Verse

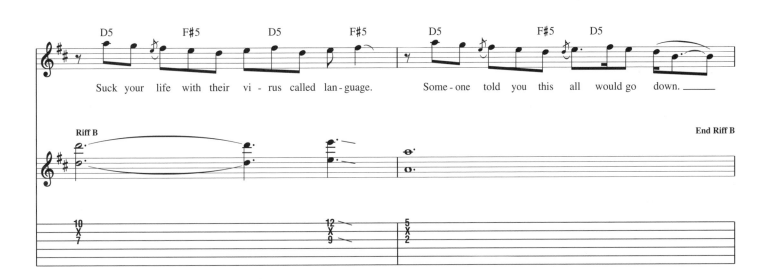

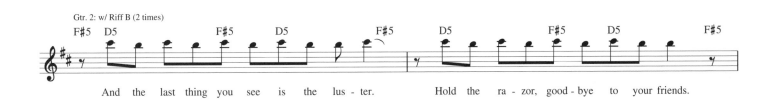

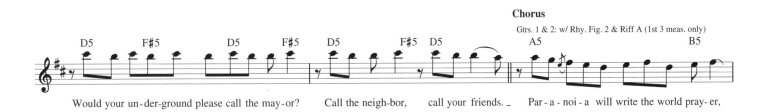

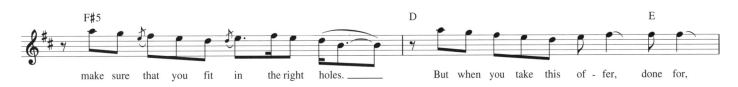

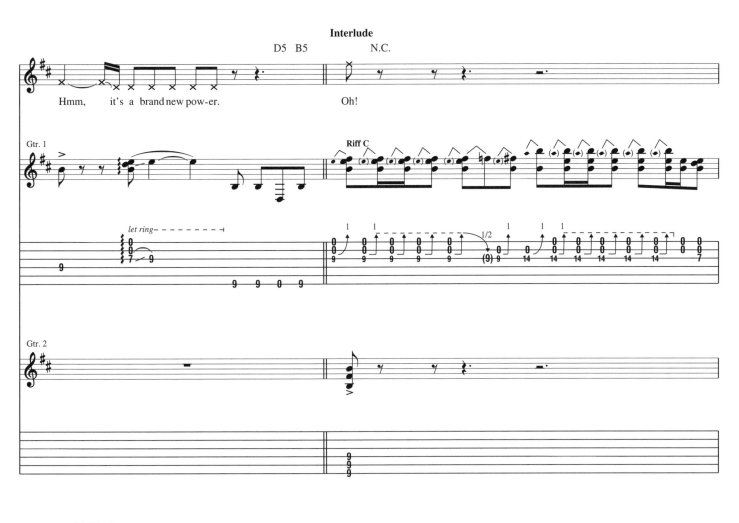

Hmm,   it's a brand new pow-er.   Oh!

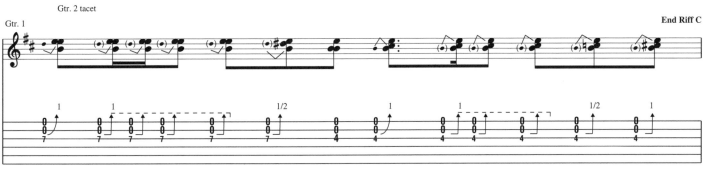

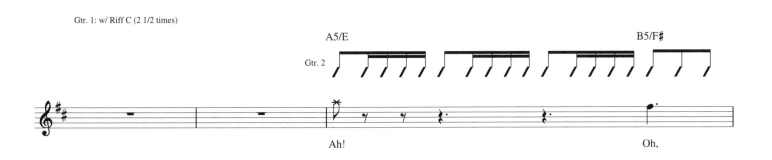

Ah!   Oh,

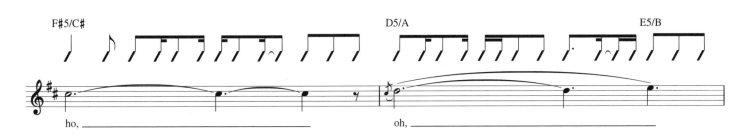

ho, _____   oh, _____

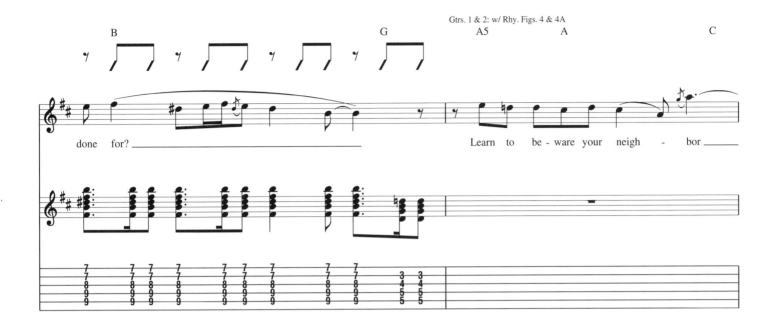

done for? _____ Learn to be - ware your neigh - bor _____

____ and the right mode. Have - n't you heard, have - n't you heard that we're ____

Outro

done for, done for, oh. _____ Oh, when I count down from ten.

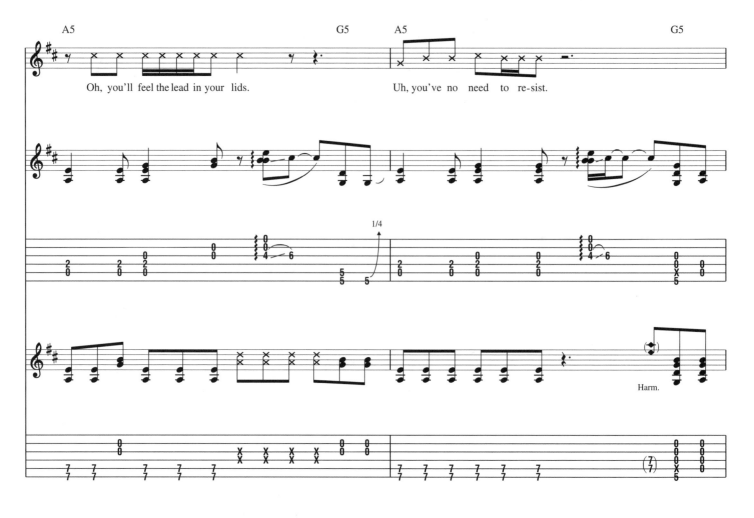

Oh, you'll feel the lead in your lids.   Uh, you've no need to re-sist.

And wake up re-freshed,   hah!

I Know We Could Be So Happy Baby (If We Wanted to Be)

Words and Music by Jeff Buckley

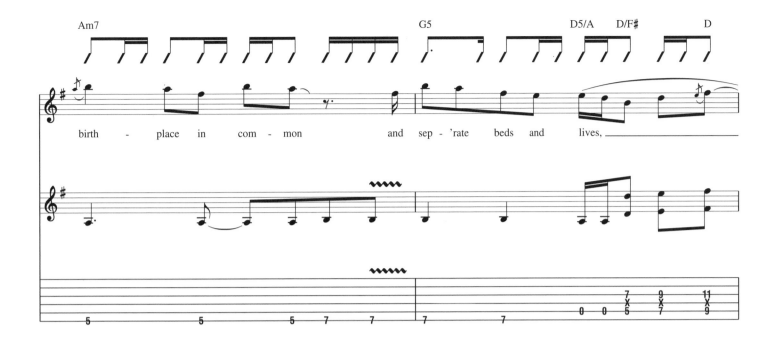

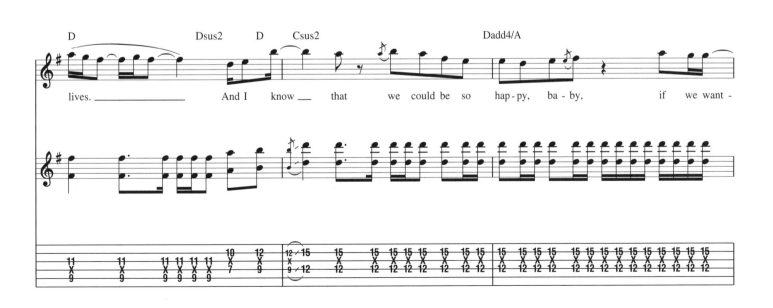

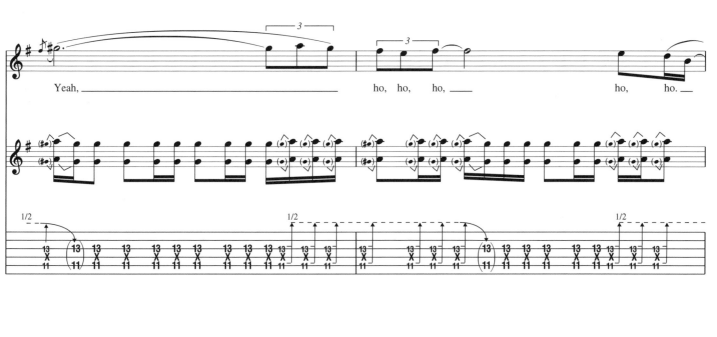

Yeah, _____ ho, ho, ho, _____ ho, ho. ___

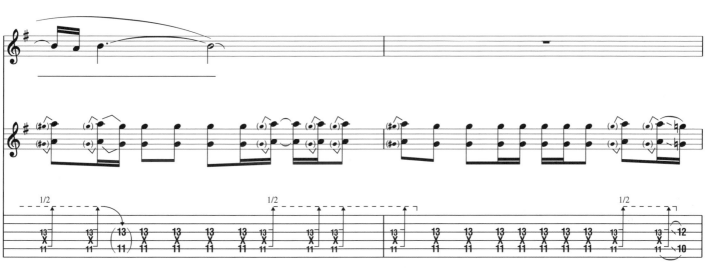

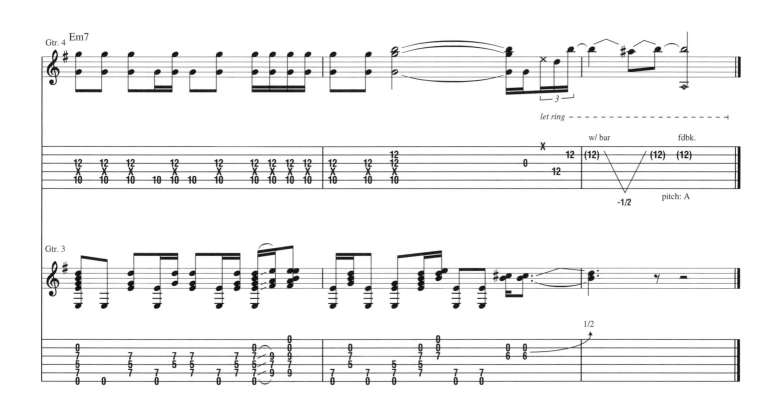

from *Mystery White Boy*

I Woke Up in a Strange Place

Words and Music by Jeff Buckley

Drop D tuning:
(low to high) D–A–D–G–B–E

Intro
Moderately ♩ = 104

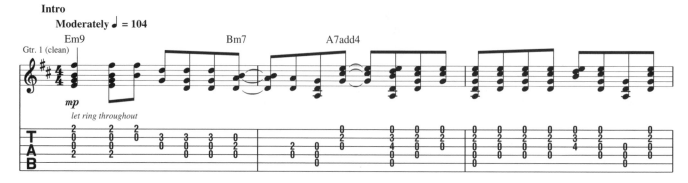

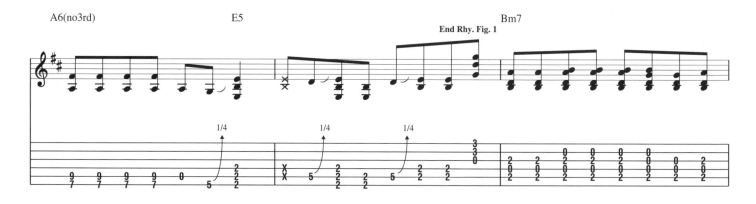

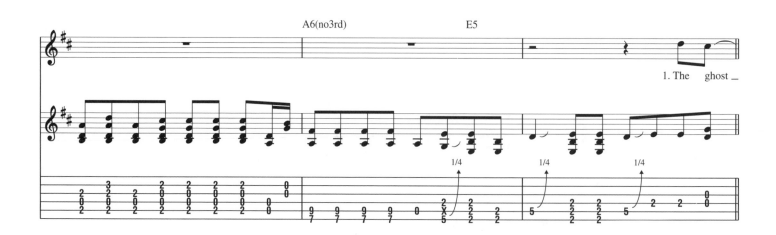

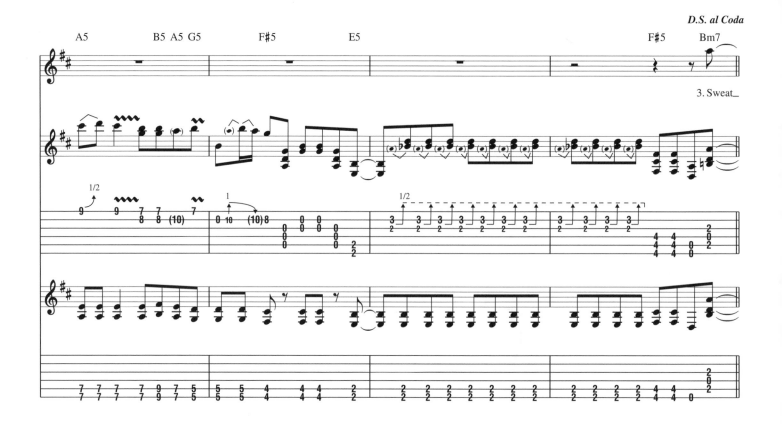

Coda

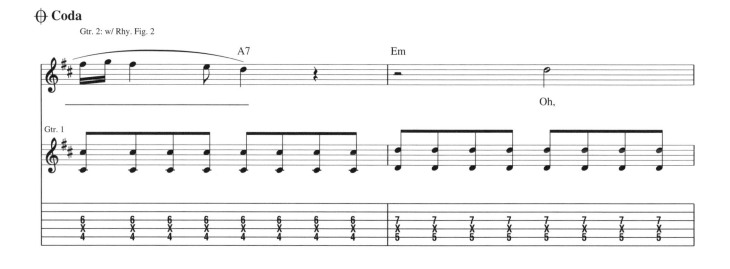

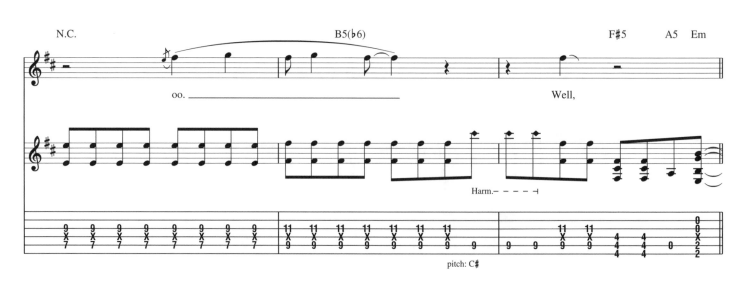

Outro Chorus

Gtrs. 1 & 2: w/ Rhy. Fig. 3

this is my sto - ry for the dis - lo - ca - ted. You're gon - na love, _ but it turned to be hat - ed.

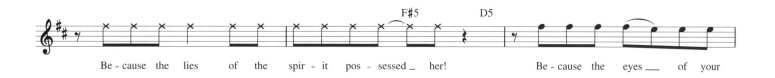

Be - cause the lies of the spir - it pos - sessed _ her! Be - cause the eyes _ of your

lov - er re - sist _ you. Lis - ten up, you keep your aim stead - y as your

tem - ple turns to kiss the pis - tol. Fate _ is gon - na find _ your love

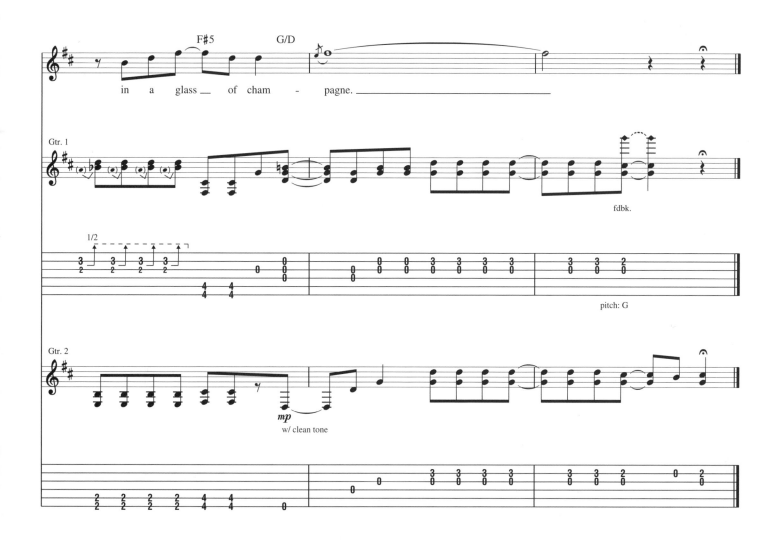

in a glass _ of cham - pagne. _

57

Jewel Box

Words and Music by Jeff Buckley

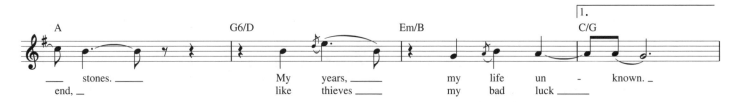

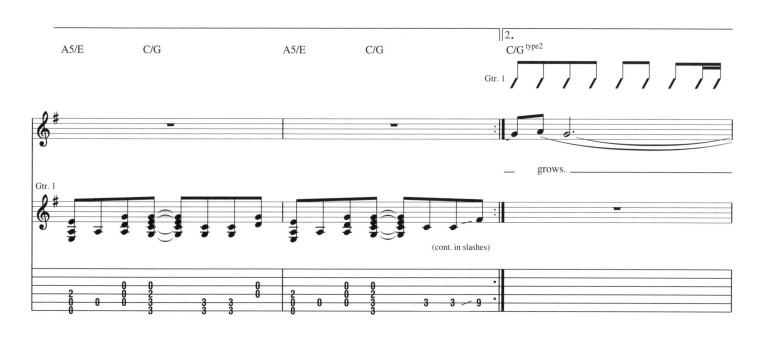

Chorus

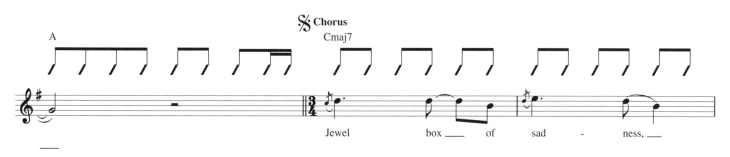

Jewel box ___ of sad - ness, ___

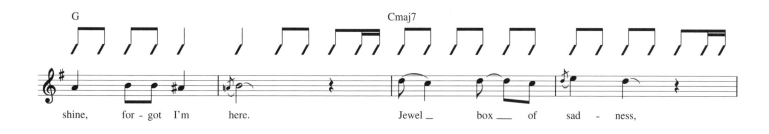

bring to catch ___ your tear. Crys - tal - lized ___ il - lu - sions, ___ they

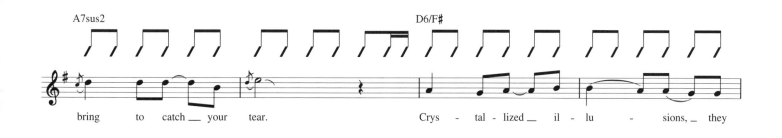

shine, for - got I'm here. Jewel ___ box ___ of sad - ness,

To Coda

bring to catch ___ your tear. ___ Oh, ___ you left some stars ___ in my ___

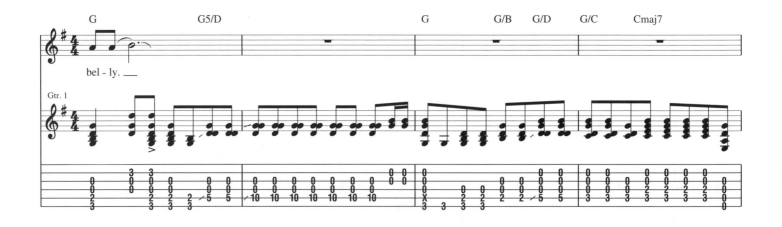

bel - ly. ___

Gtr. 1

Verse

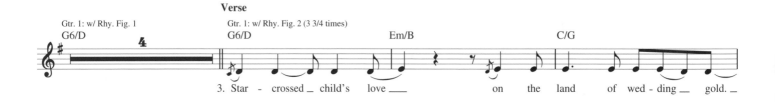

3. Star - crossed ___ child's love ___ on the land of wed - ding ___ gold. ___

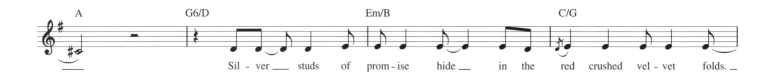

___ Sil - ver ___ studs of prom - ise hide ___ in the red crushed vel - vet folds. ___

___ In - ac - tion, in - ten - tion, like em - er - alds ___ I

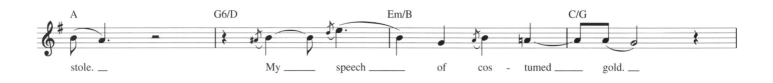

stole. ___ My ___ speech ___ of cos - tumed ___ gold. ___

D.S. al Coda

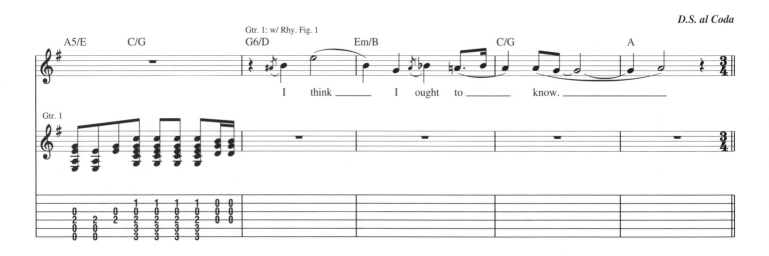

I think ___ I ought to ___ know. ___

Gtr. 1

from *Grace*

Last Goodbye

Words and Music by Jeff Buckley

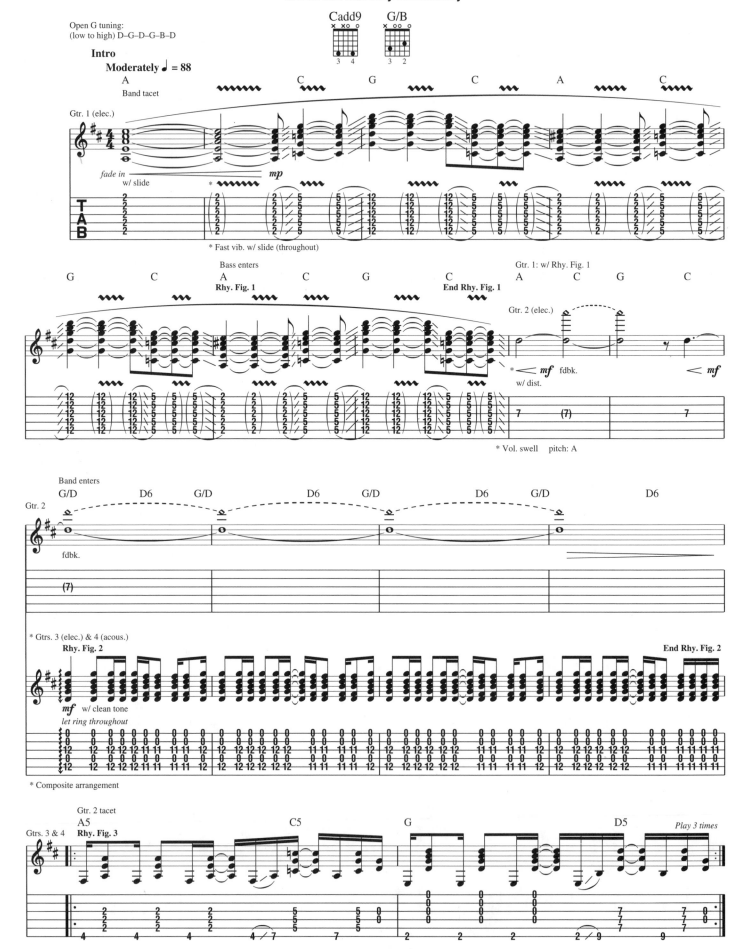

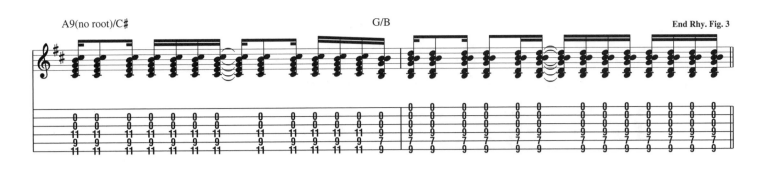

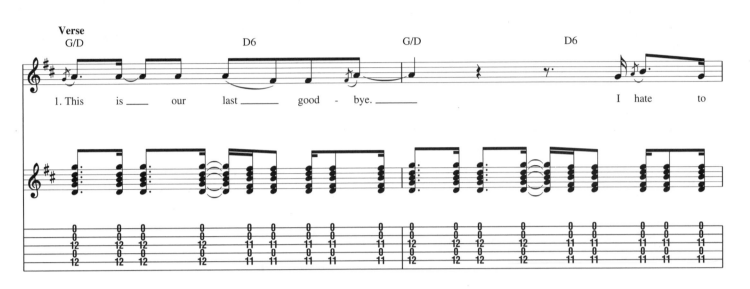

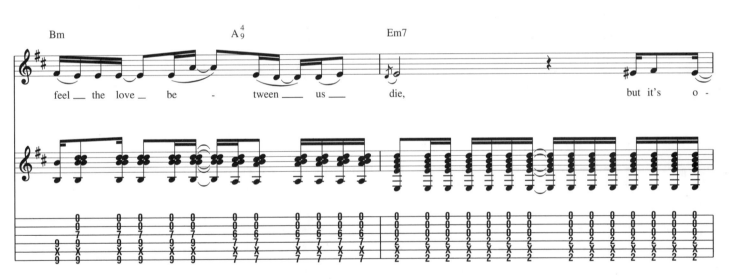

64

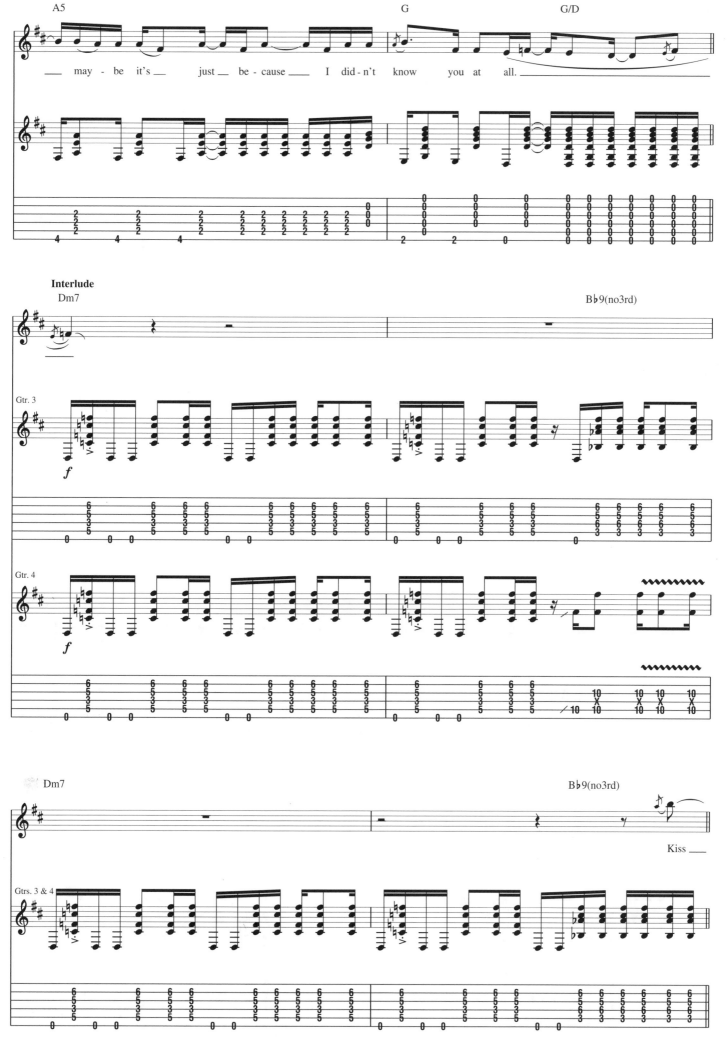

may - be it's __ just __ be - cause __ I did-n't know you at all. __

Interlude

Kiss __

Bridge

me, please kiss me, but kiss me out of de- sire, babe, and not

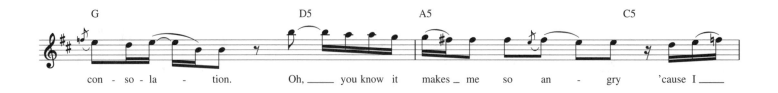

con- so- la- tion. Oh, you know it makes me so an- gry 'cause I

know that in time I'll on- ly make you cry. This is our last good- bye.

Interlude

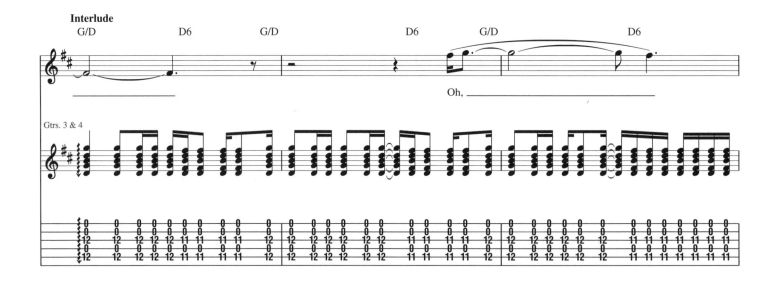

Oh,

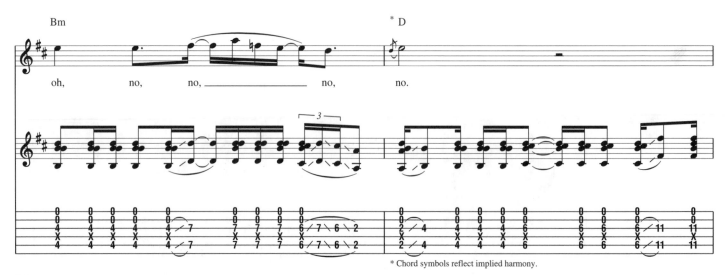

oh, no, no, no, no.

* Chord symbols reflect implied harmony.

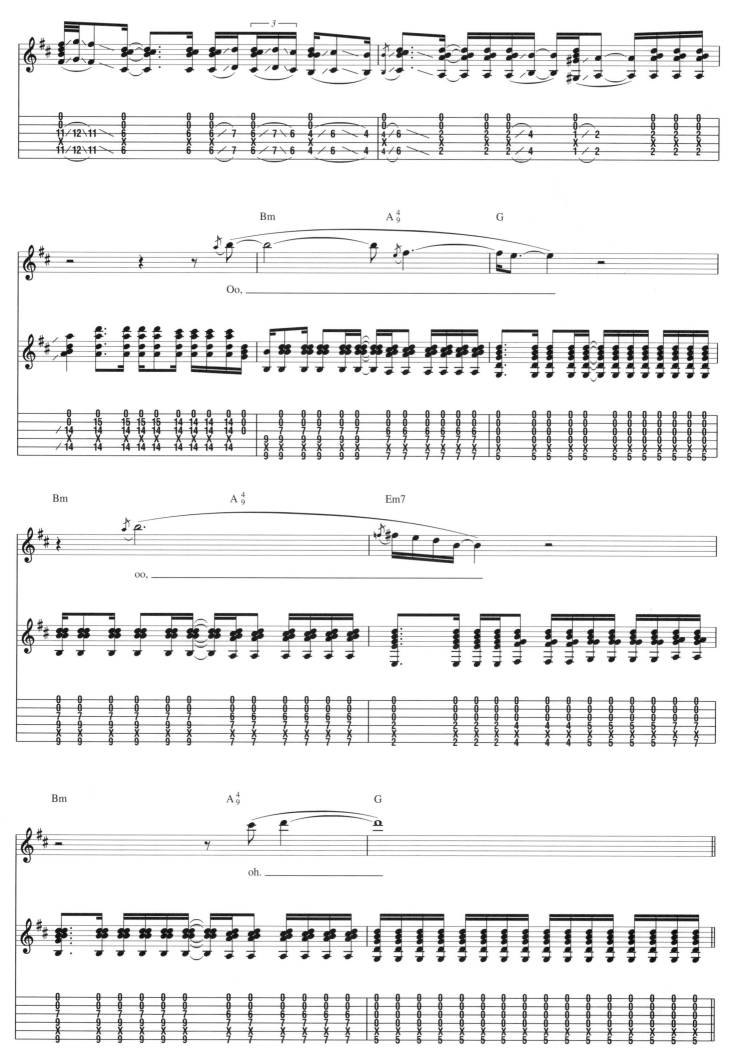

Interlude
Gtrs. 3 & 4: w/ Rhy. Fig. 3 (1st 4 meas. only)

Oo, _____ you did-n't know. _____   4. Well, the

Verse

bells_ out _ in the church tow - er chime, _____   burn - in'_

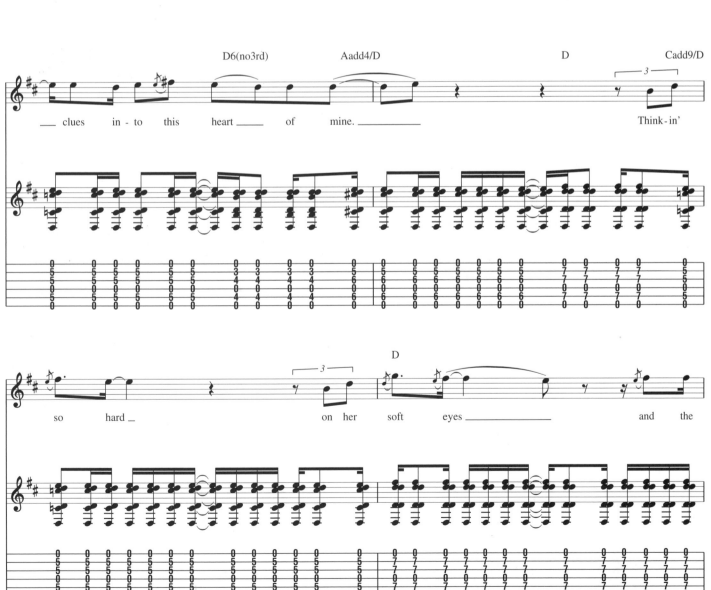

_ clues in - to this heart _____ of mine. _____   Think - in'

so   hard _   on her soft eyes _____   and the

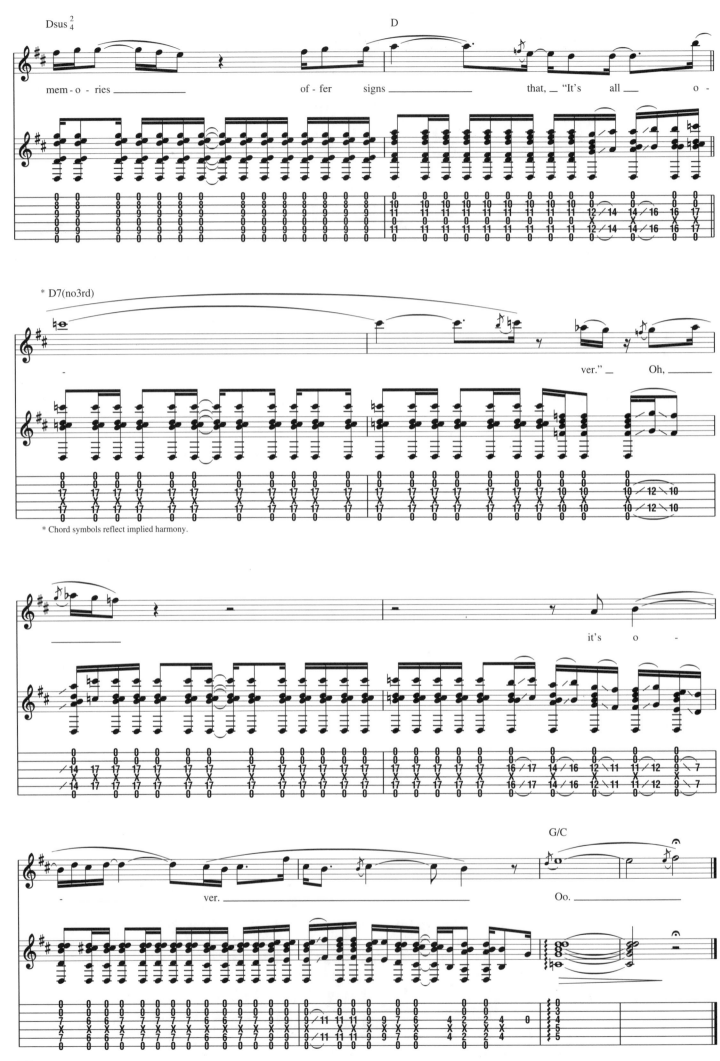

* Chord symbols reflect implied harmony.

from *Grace*

Lover, You Should've Come Over

Words and Music by Jeff Buckley

smiles when ___ I slept so soft a - gainst her. It's _____ nev - er o -

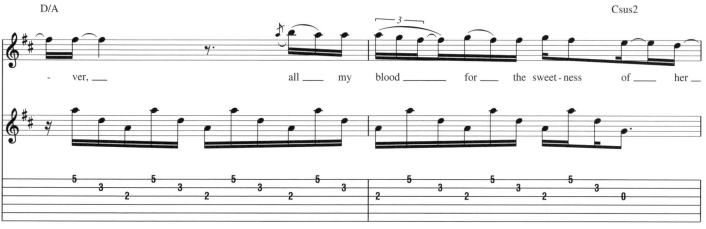

- ver, ___ all ___ my blood _____ for ___ the sweet - ness of ___ her ___

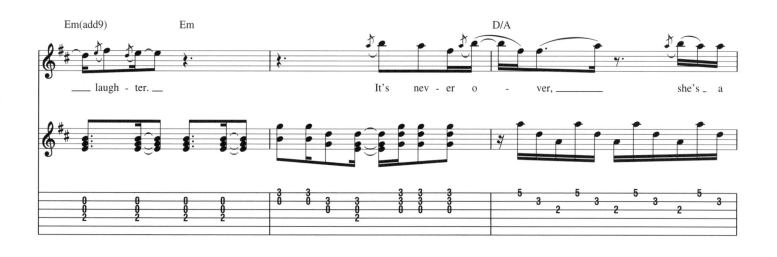

___ laugh - ter. ___ It's nev - er o - ver, _____ she's _ a

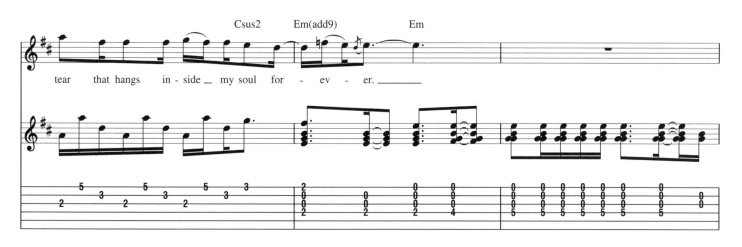

tear that hangs in - side ___ my soul for - ev - er. _____

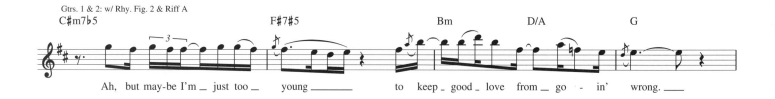

Gtrs. 1 & 2: w/ Rhy. Fig. 2 & Riff A

C#m7b5   F#7#5   Bm   D/A   G

Ah, but may-be I'm _ just too _ young _____ to keep _ good _ love from _ go - in' wrong. _____

Outro chorus

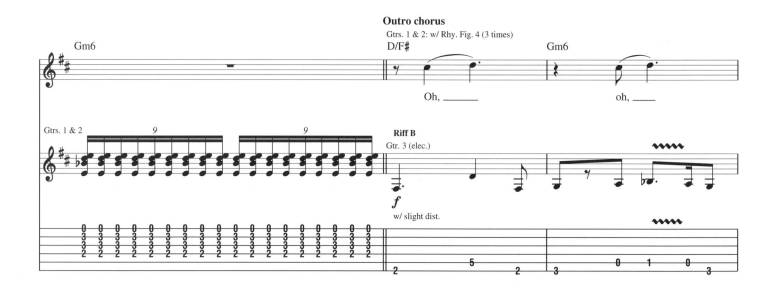

Gtrs. 1 & 2: w/ Rhy. Fig. 4 (3 times)

Gm6   D/F#   Gm6

Oh, _____   oh, _____

Gtrs. 1 & 2

Riff B
Gtr. 3 (elec.)

f

w/ slight dist.

A⁶₉   G6/B   Aadd9/C#   Cmaj7/E   D⁶₉

oh, _____   oh, _____   oh. _____

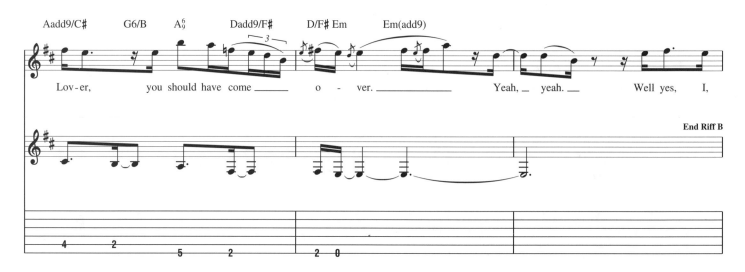

Aadd9/C#   G6/B   A⁶₉   Dadd9/F#   D/F# Em   Em(add9)

Lov-er,   you should have come _____ o - ver. _____ Yeah, _ yeah.   Well yes, I,

End Riff B

Gtr. 3: w/ Riff B (2 times)

I feel __ too __ young to hold __ on, and I'm much too old to break free and

run. __ Too __ deaf, dumb, and blind to see __ the dam-age I've __ done. Sweet __

lov - er, __ you, you should-'ve come _ o - ver. Oh love, _ well I'm wait-ing for you.

Lov - er, __ lov - er, love, __ lov - er, __ love, love, _ love, love,

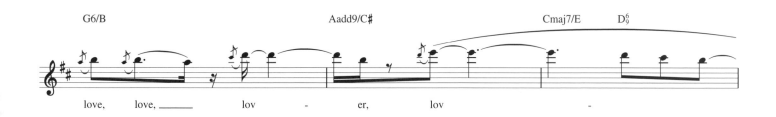

love, love, __ lov - er, lov -

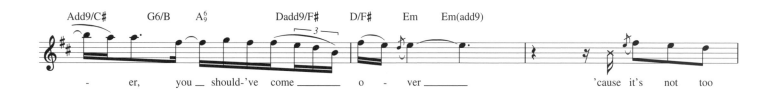

- er, you _ should-'ve come __ o - ver __ 'cause it's not too

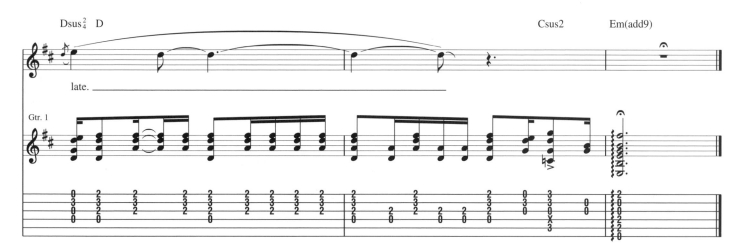

late. __

Gtr. 1

from *Grace*

Mojo Pin

Words and Music by Jeff Buckley and Gary Lucas

Drop D tuning:
(low to high) D–A–D–G–B–E

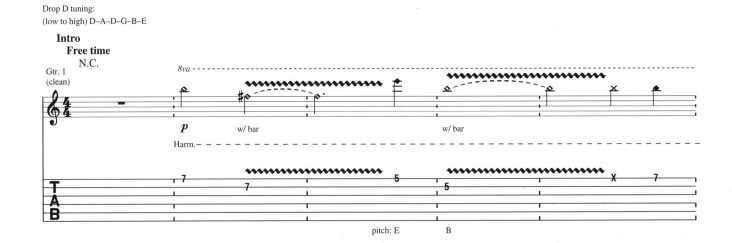

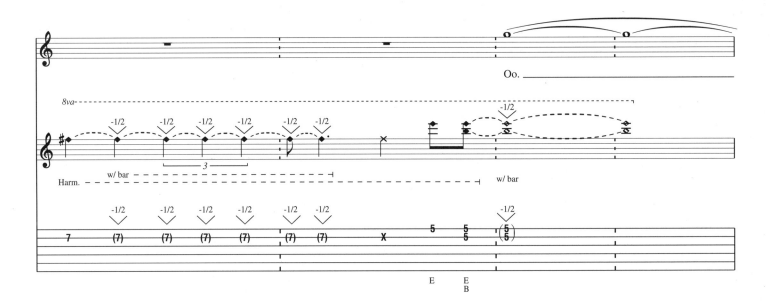

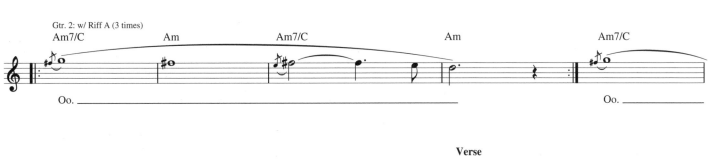

Oo. _____

Oo. _____

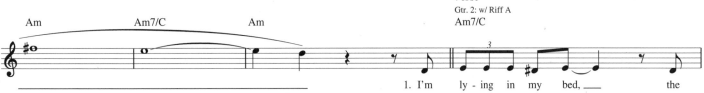

Oo. _____

1. I'm ly - ing in my bed, ___ the

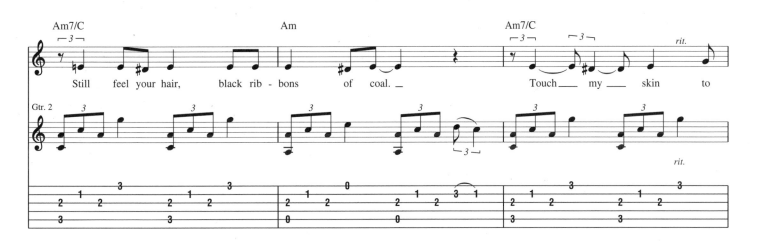

blan - ket is warm. _ This ___ bod - y will nev - er be safe ___ from harm. _

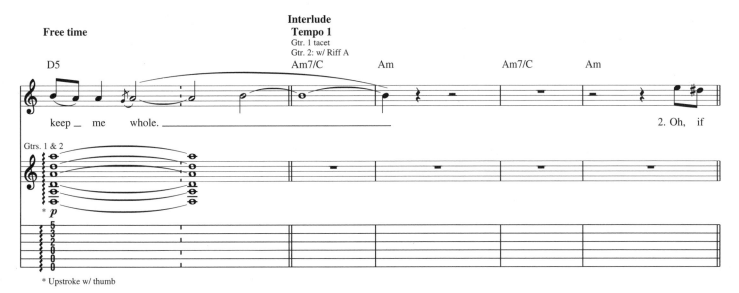

Still feel your hair, black rib - bons of coal. _ Touch ___ my ___ skin to

keep ___ me whole. _____ 2. Oh, if

* Upstroke w/ thumb

𝄋 **Verse**

Gtr. 2: w/ Riff A (1 3/4 times)

on - ly you'd come back to me, if you laid at ___ my ___ side, _____

_ a - gain _____ from the rhyth - m scream - ing ___ down ___ from heav - en.

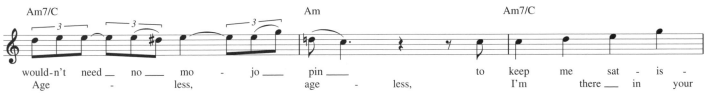

⊕ Coda 2

Interlude
Faster ♩ = 97

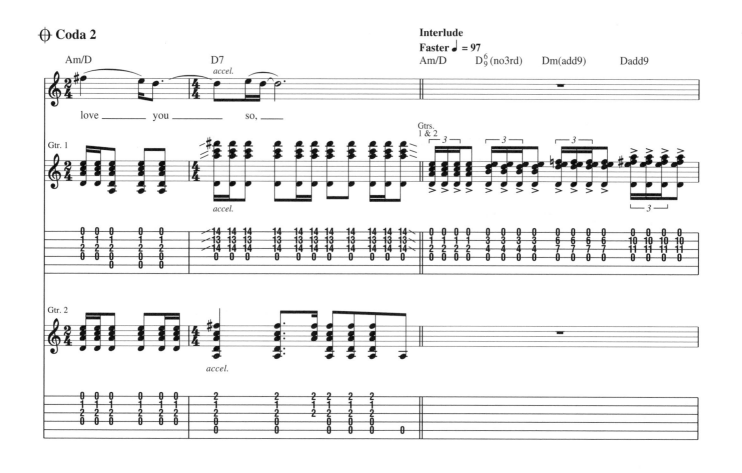

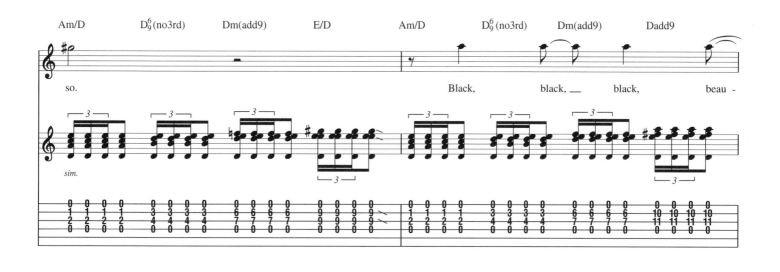

Free time

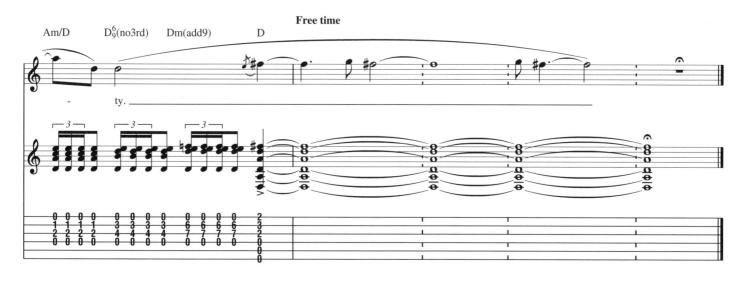

from *Mystery White Boy*

Moodswing Whiskey

Words and Music by Jeff Buckley and Michael Tighe

Gtr. 1: w/ Rhy. Fig. 1

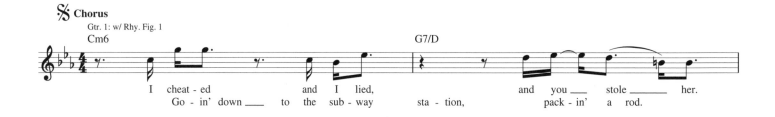

I cheat-ed and I lied, and you __ stole __ her.
Go-in' down __ to the sub-way sta-tion, pack-in' a rod.

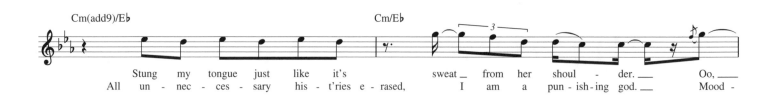

Stung my tongue just like it's sweat __ from her shoul-der. __ Oo, __
All un-nec-ces-sa-ry his-t'ries e-rased, I am a pun-ish-ing god. Mood-

To Coda ⊕

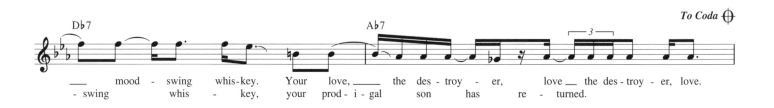

__ mood-swing whis-key. Your love, __ the des-troy-er, love __ the des-troy-er, love.
-swing whis-key, your prod-i-gal son has re-turned.

Bridge

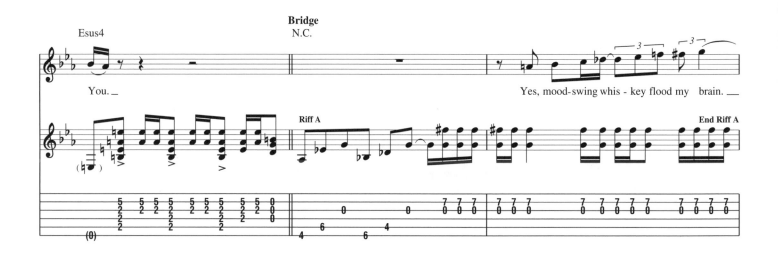

You. __ Yes, mood-swing whis-key flood my brain. __

Riff A   End Riff A

Gtr. 1: w/ Riff A (6 times)

__ On - ly you __ could wreck this chain. __

I need her in my __ bed a-gain. __ Yeah, __ yeah, __ yeah, __ yeah.

D.S. al Coda

Play 3 times

__ Yeah, yeah, __ yeah, __ yeah, yeah.

Coda

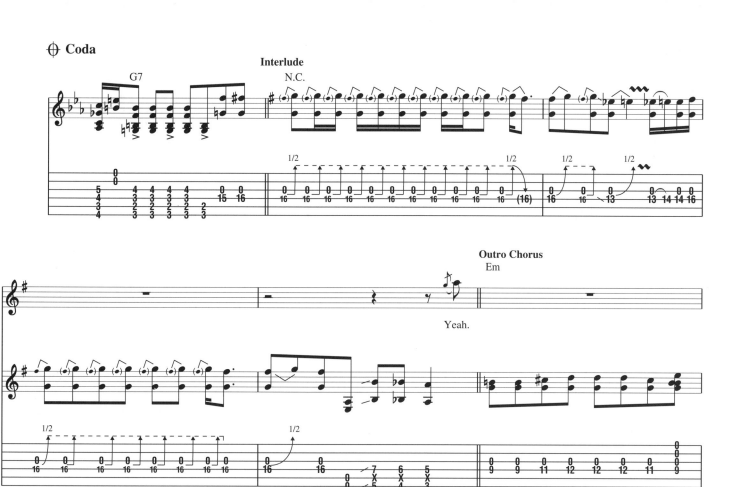

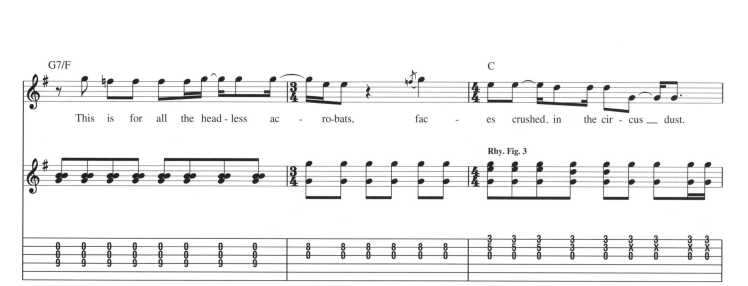

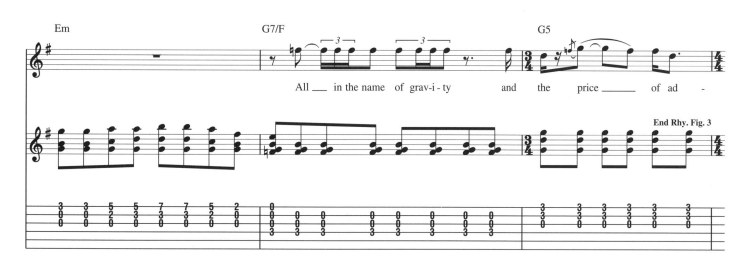

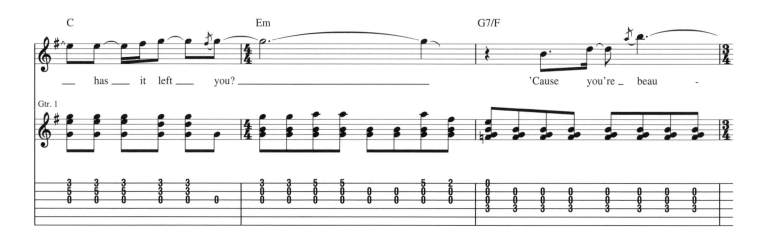

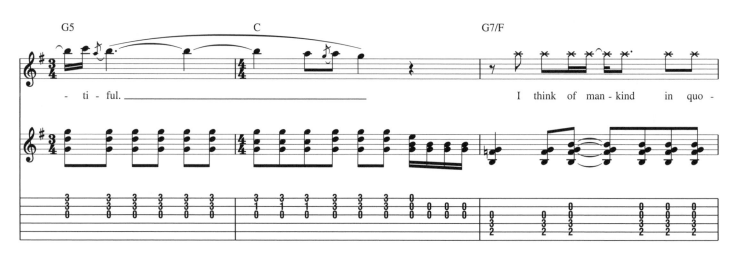

Morning Theft

Words and Music by Jeff Buckley

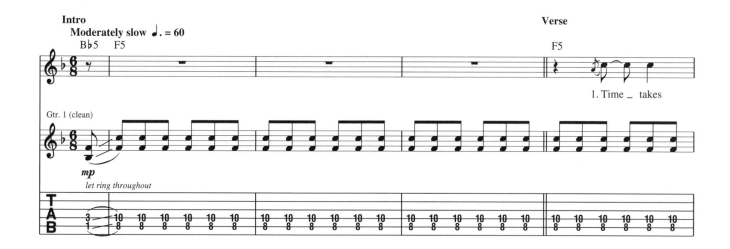

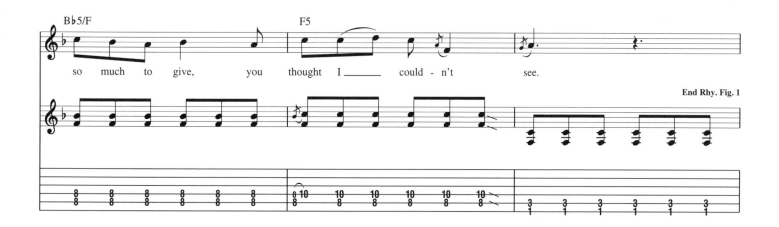

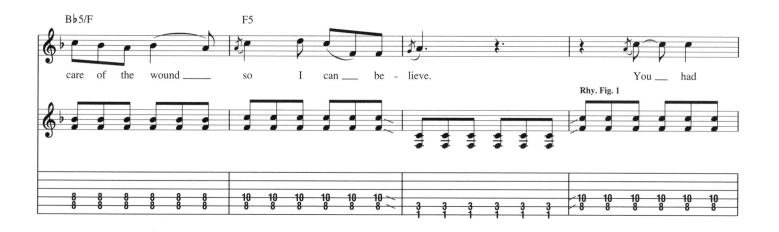

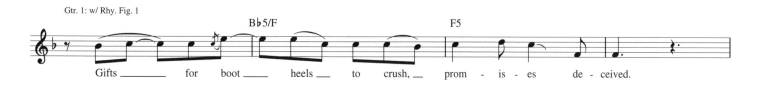

I had to send it a-way to bring us back a-gain. ___

Verse

Gtr. 1: w/ Rhy. Fig. 1 (2 times)

2. Your eyes and bod — y bright — en si — lent wat — ers deep.

Your pre — cious daugh — ter ___ in the oth — er ___ room, ___ a-sleep.

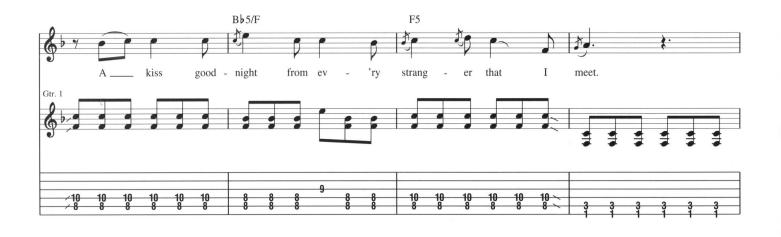

A ___ kiss good — night from ev — 'ry strang — er that I meet.

I had to send it a-way to bring us back a-gain. ___

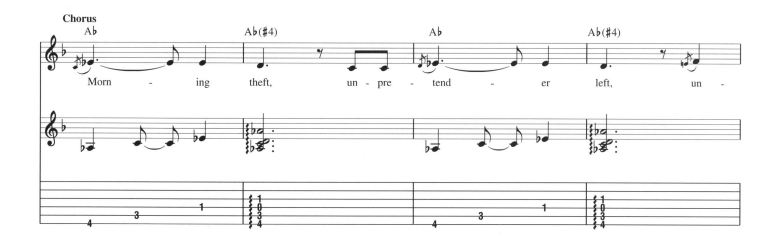

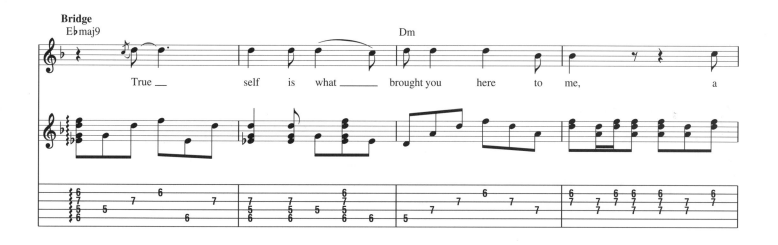

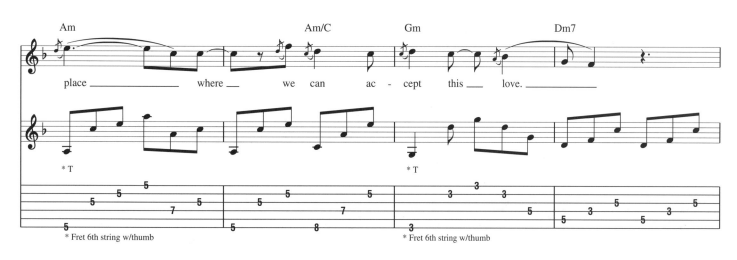

Friend - ship bat - tered down __ by use - less his - to - ry, un - ex -

am - ined fail - ure, _____ oh. __

* Fret 6th string w/ thumb   * Fret 6th string w/ thumb

Interlude

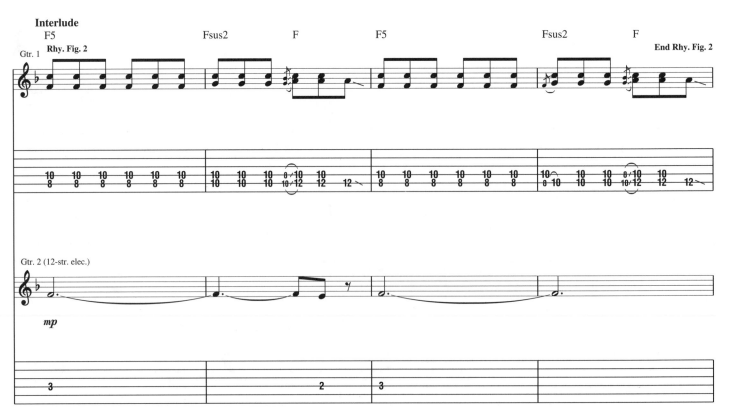

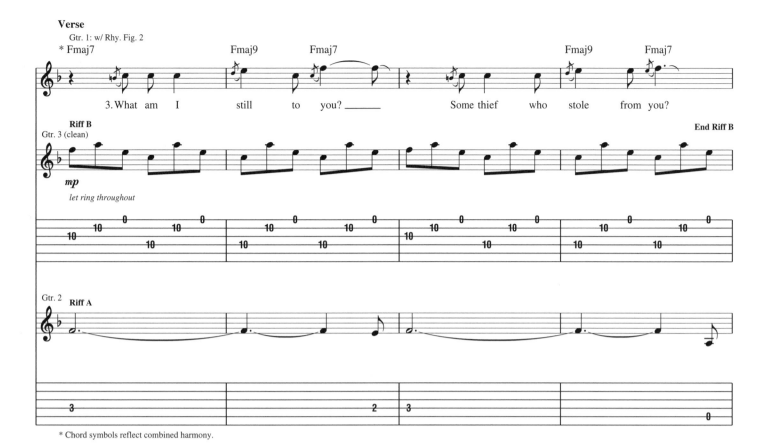

brings us to who we need, a place where we can save

a heart that beats __ as __ both si - phon __ and res - er - voir.

You're a wom - an, I'm a calf. You're a win - dow, I'm a knife.

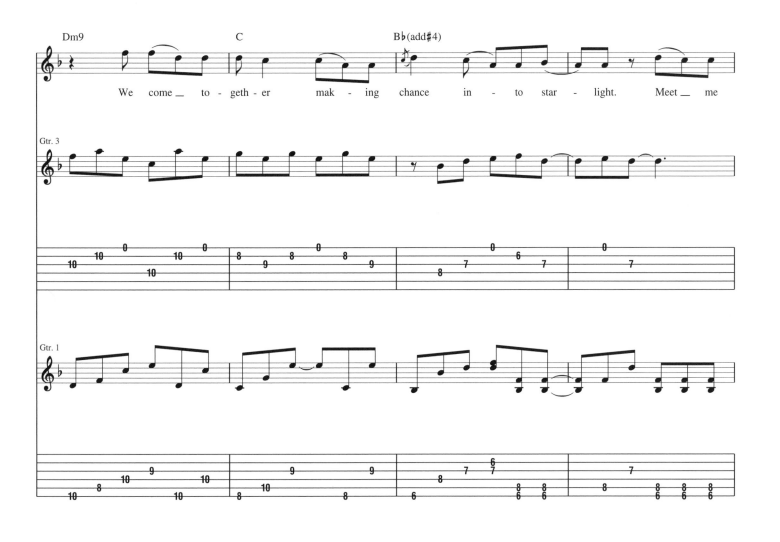

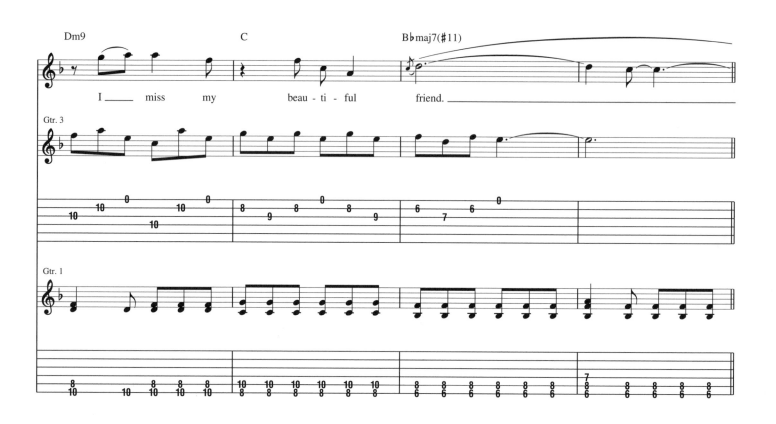

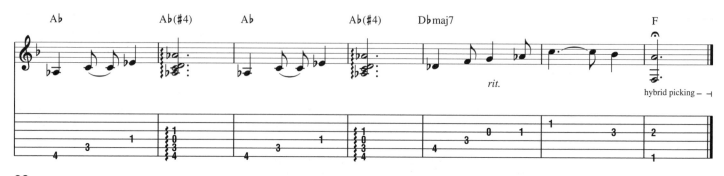

New Year's Prayer

Words and Music by Jeff Buckley

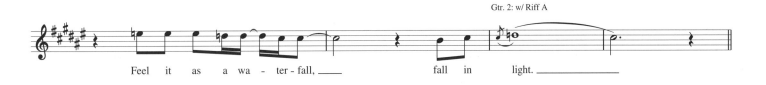

Feel it as a wa - ter - fall, ___ fall in light. ___

Chorus

Oh, _____ fall in light, ___ fall in light, ___ fall in light. Oo, _

mf

_____ fall in light, ___ fall in light, ___ fall in light. Grow in _

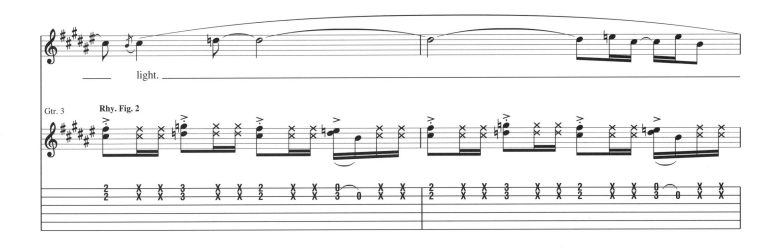

___ light. _____

Gtr. 3

Rhy. Fig. 2

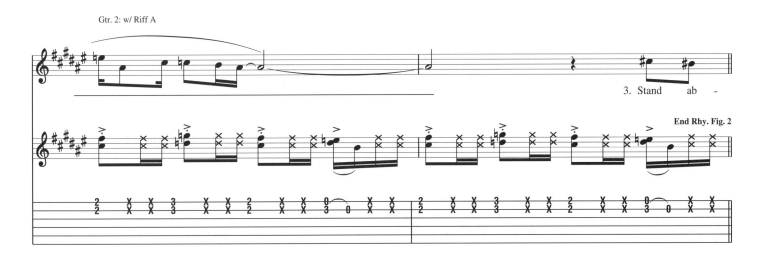

_____ 3. Stand ab -

End Rhy. Fig. 2

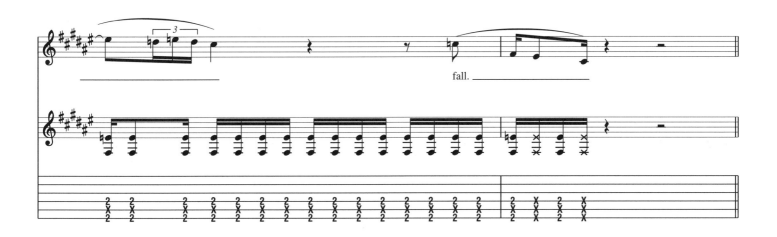

Chorus

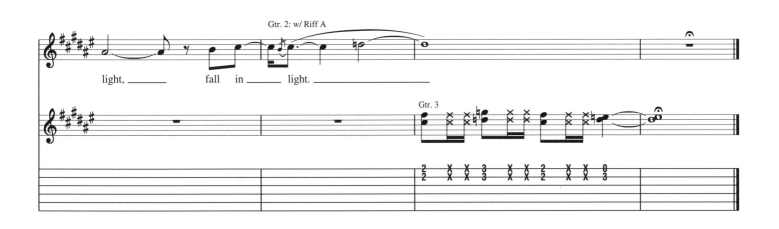

Nightmares by the Sea

Words and Music by Jeff Buckley

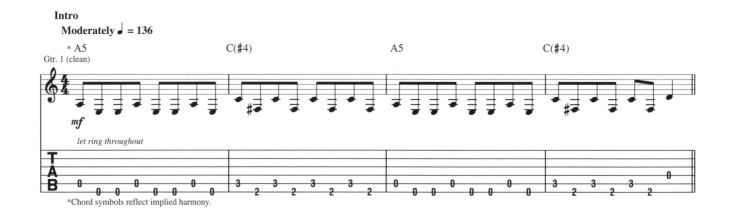

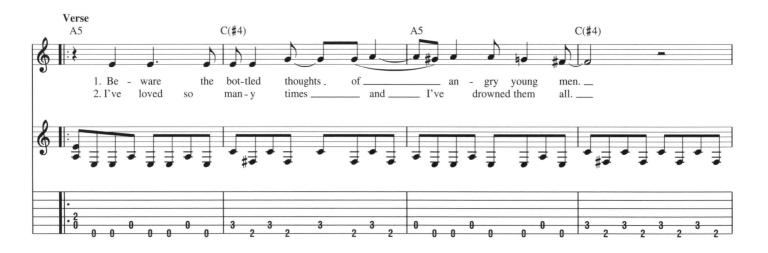

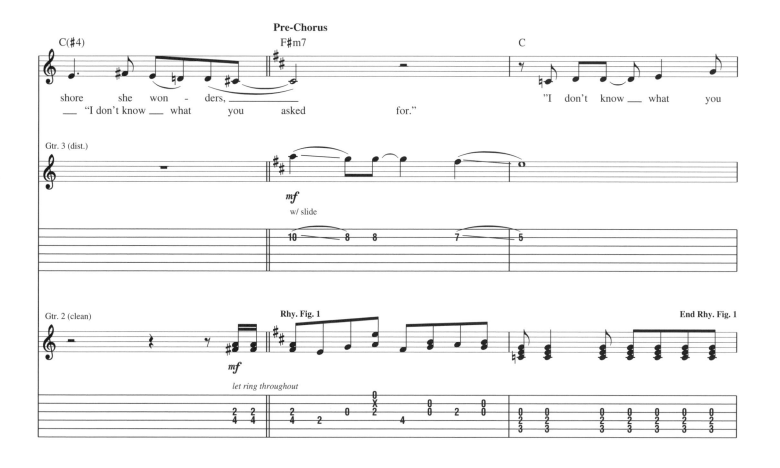

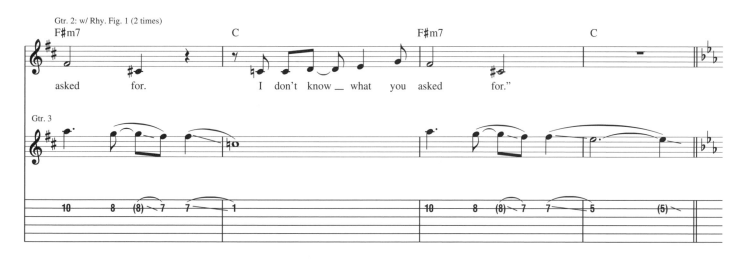

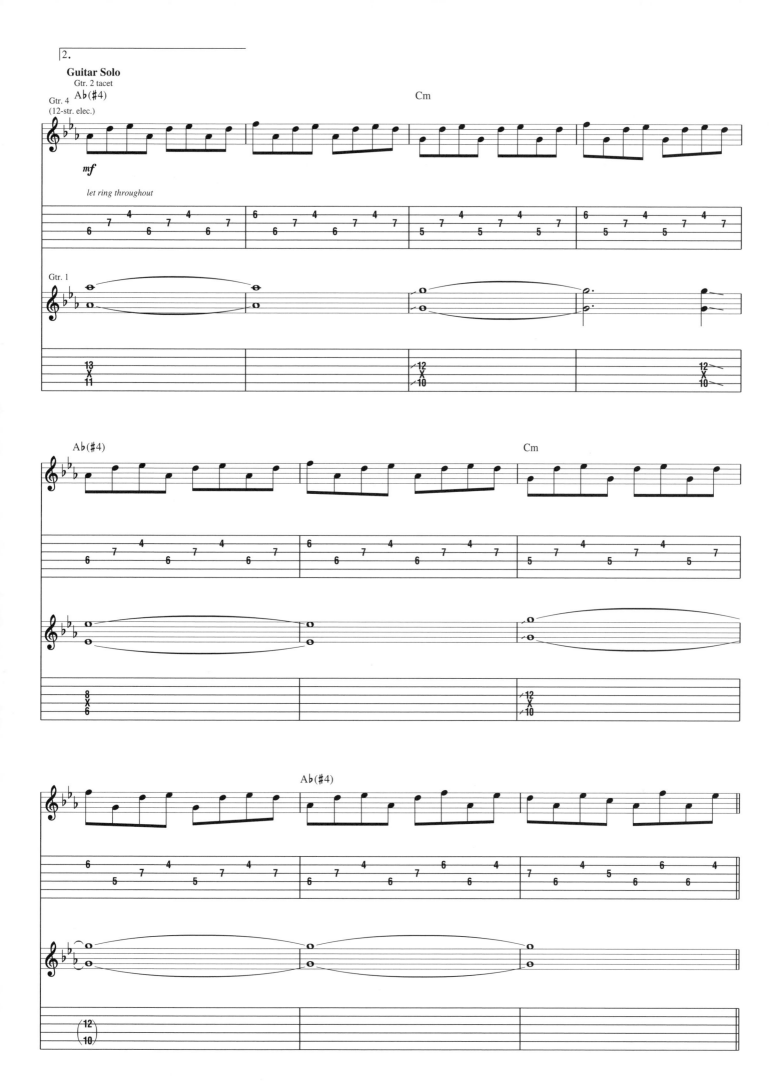

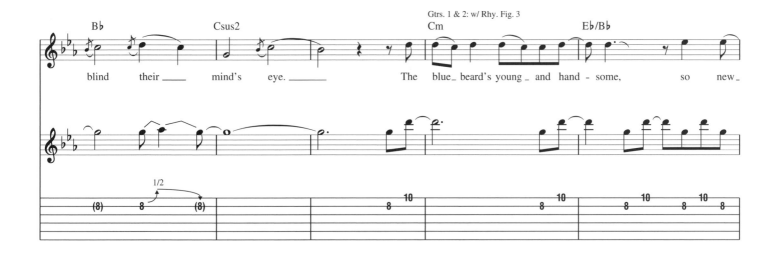

Gtrs. 1 & 2: w/ Rhy. Fig. 3

blind their ___ mind's eye. ___ The blue_ beard's young _ and hand - some, so new_

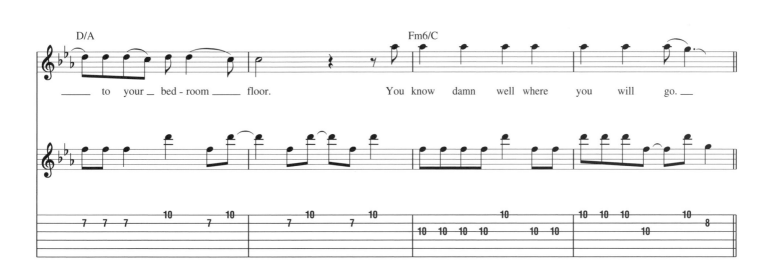

___ to your _ bed - room ___ floor. You know damn well where you will go. ___

Outro

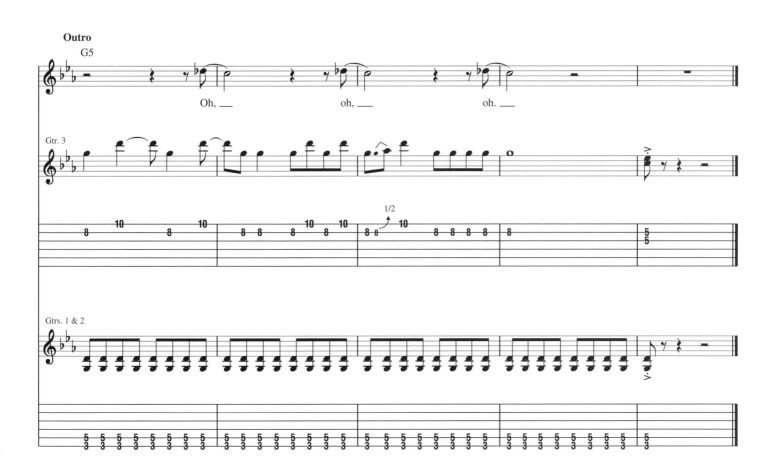

Oh, ___ oh, ___ oh. ___

Gtr. 3

Gtrs. 1 & 2

Opened Once

Words and Music by Jeff Buckley

* Chord symbols reflect implied harmony.

The Sky Is a Landfill

Words and Music by Jeff Buckley and Michael Tighe

Drop D tuning:
(low to high) D–A–D–G–B–E

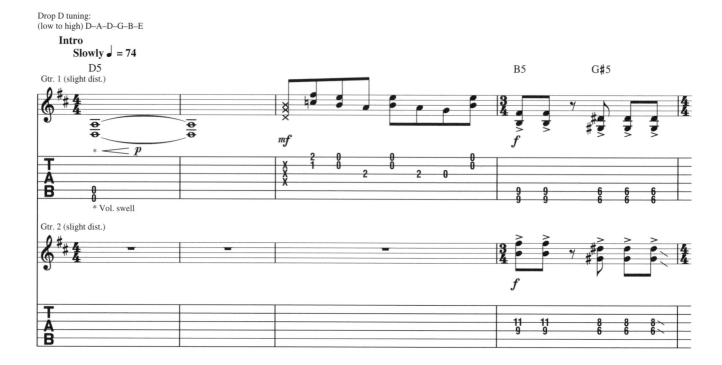

* Chord symbols reflect combined harmony.

We cast our fun-er-al rose _ in - side _ and bur-y the need to prove. _

Well, our mu-ti-la-tion is to gain from the sys-tem. _____

End Rhy. Fig. 2

End Rhy. Fig. 2A

Verse

Gtr. 1: w/ Rhy. Fig. 1

Gtr. 2 tacet

2. Oh, _____ turn your head a - way _____ from the screen. Oh peo - ple,

Gtr. 2

it will tell you noth-ing _____ more. Don't suck the milk ___ of flac-cid Bill ___ K.

Pub-lic's emp-ty prom-ise to the peo-ple that the pub-lic can ig-nore. __

Gtr. 3

Gtr. 2 | **Rhy. Fill 1** | **End Rhy. Fill 1**

Pre-Chorus

Gtr. 3 tacet
Gtrs. 1 & 2: w/ Rhy. Figs. 2 & 2A

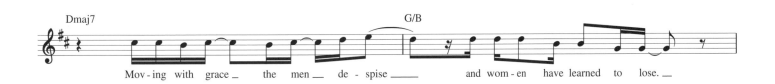

This way of life ___ is so ___ de-vised _____ to snuff out the mind ___ that moves. __

Mov-ing with grace ___ the men ___ de-spise _____ and wom-en have learned to lose. __

Throw off your shame or be a slave to the sys-tem.

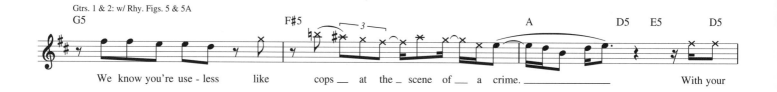

We know you're use-less like cops __ at the _ scene of __ a crime. _____ With your

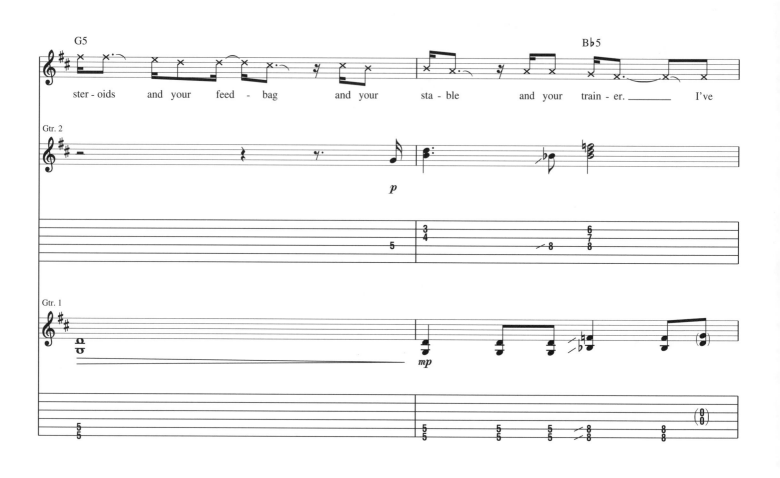

ster-oids and your feed-bag and your sta-ble and your train-er. _____ I've

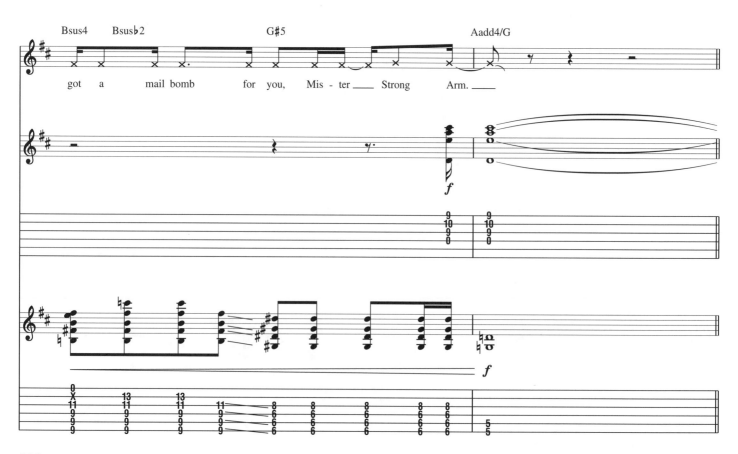

got a mail bomb for you, Mis-ter __ Strong Arm. __

Verse

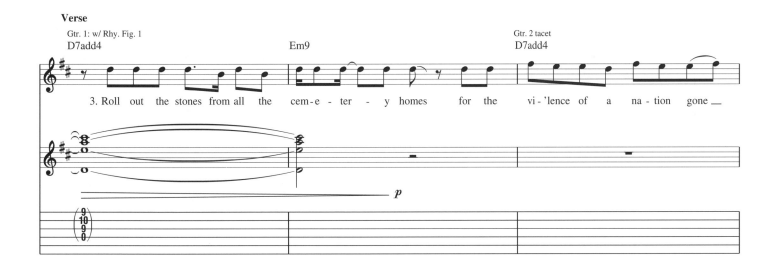

Gtr. 1: w/ Rhy. Fig. 1

Gtr. 2 tacet

D7add4   Em9   D7add4

3. Roll out the stones from all the cem-e-ter-y homes for the vi-'lence of a na-tion gone ___

p

G5   D7add4

by.   For the pol-i-tics ___ of weak-ness   and the

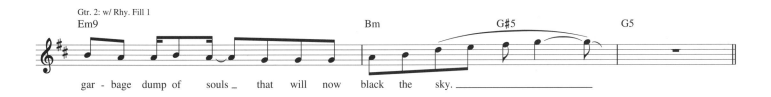

Gtr. 2: w/ Rhy. Fill 1

Em9   Bm   G#5   G5

gar-bage dump of souls ___ that will now black the sky. _____

Pre-Chorus

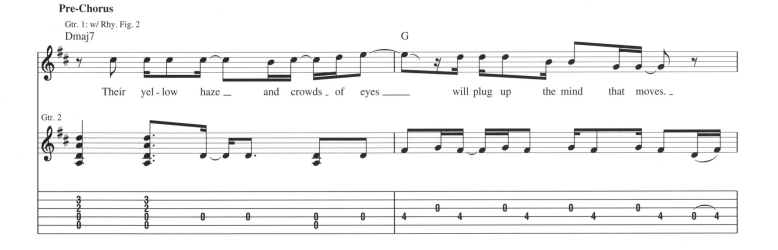

Gtr. 1: w/ Rhy. Fig. 2

Dmaj7   G

Their yel-low haze ___ and crowds __ of eyes _____ will plug up the mind that moves. _

Gtr. 2

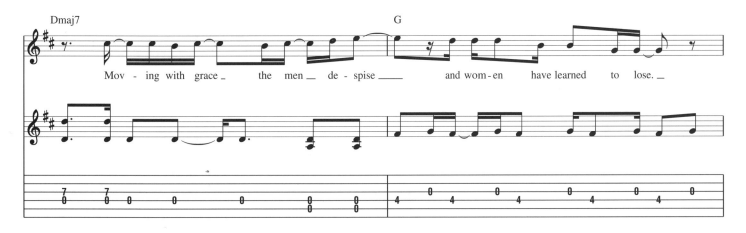

Dmaj7   G

Mov-ing with grace __ the men __ de-spise _____ and wom-en have learned to lose. _

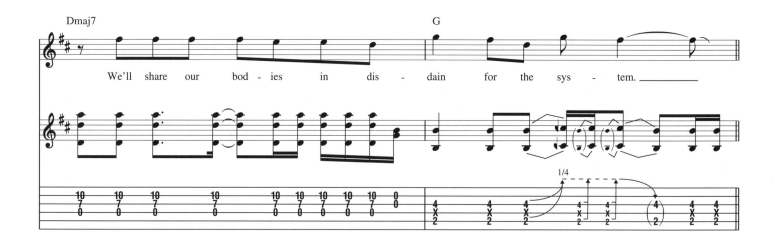

We'll share our bod-ies in dis-dain for the sys-tem. _____

Chorus

Gtrs. 1 & 2: w/ Rhy. Figs. 3 & 3A (3 times)

D7

Oh, ___ we see you take an-oth-er drag.

One na-tion bends to kiss ___ the hag.

The sky is a land-fill. _____

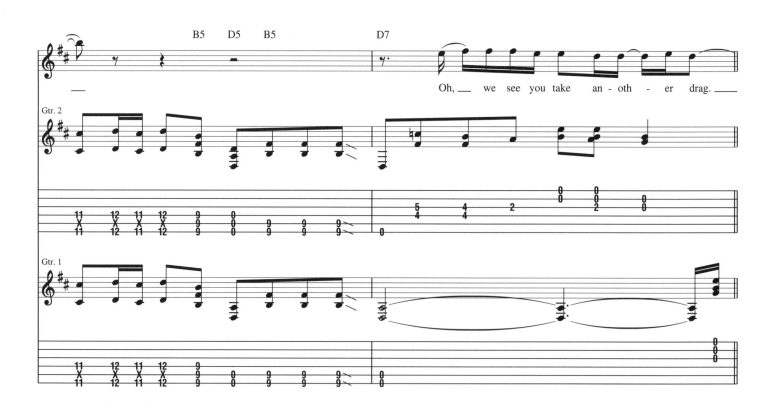

B5   D5   B5   D7

Oh, ___ we see you take an-oth-er drag. _____

Gtr. 2

Gtr. 1

Interlude

Gtr. 1: w/ Riff A (2 times)
Gtr. 2: w/ Rhy. Fig. 4 (4 times)

B5 D5 B5   D5 B5   D5 B5   D5   B5

_____   We see you take an-oth-er drag. _____   Oh, I have no ___ fear of this ma-chine!

from *Grace*

So Real

Words and Music by Jeff Buckley and Michael Tighe

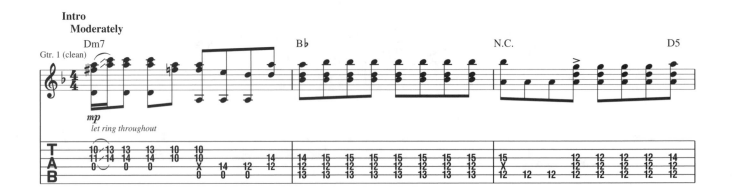

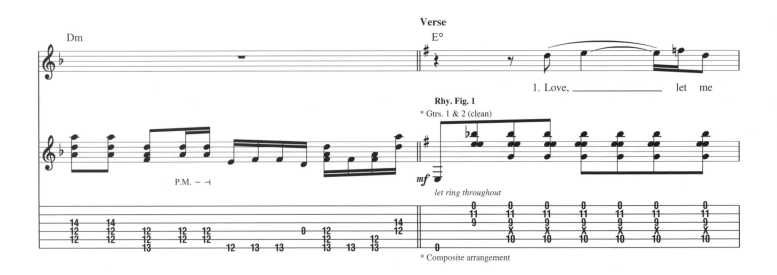

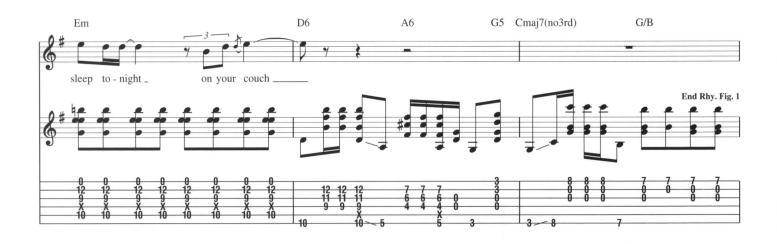

cracks 'cause I thought I'd hurt my moth-er. __

And I could-n't a-wake from the night-

D.S. al Coda 1

mare   that sucked me in   and pulled me un - der, __   pulled me un - der, __   oh.

⊕ Coda 1

Guitar Solo

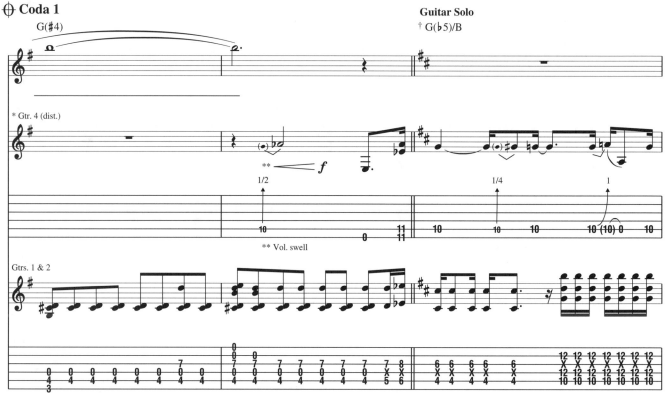

* Amplified acoustic (w/ dist.) w/ fretboard rubbed against speaker cabinet, creating sound of pitchbends (arr. for conventionally played dist. elec.)

† Chord symbols reflect overall harmony.

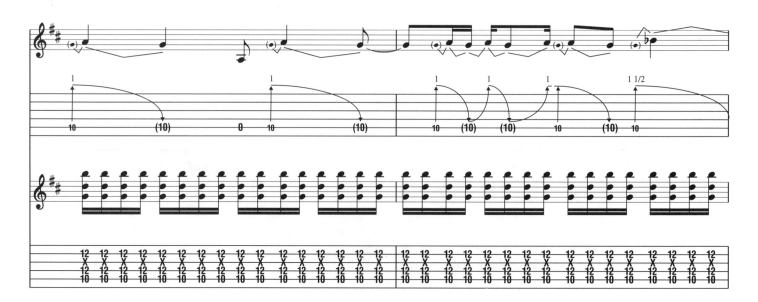

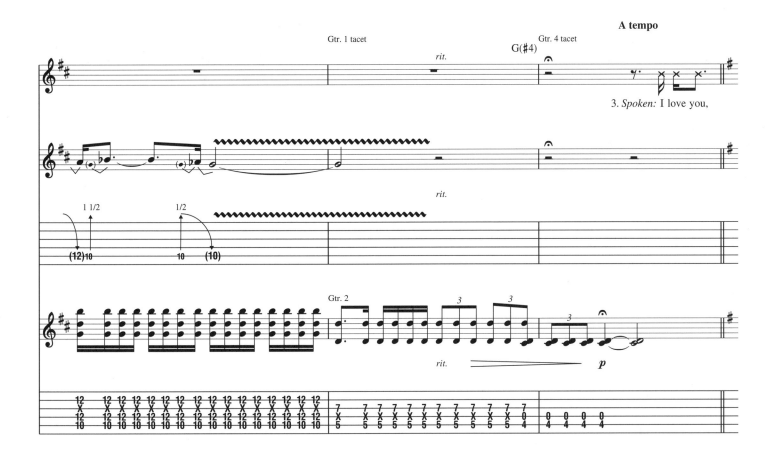

A tempo

Gtr. 1 tacet   Gtr. 4 tacet

G(♯4)

rit.

3. *Spoken:* I love you,

Gtr. 2

rit.

p

Verse

Gtrs. 1 & 2: w/ Rhy. Fig. 1 (2 times)

E°   Em   D6   A6   G5   Cmaj7(no3rd)   G/B

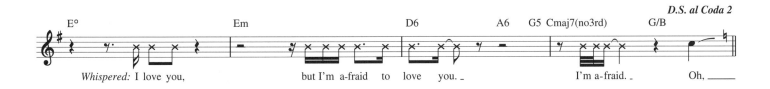

but I'm a - fraid to love you.

D.S. al Coda 2

E°   Em   D6   A6   G5   Cmaj7(no3rd)   G/B

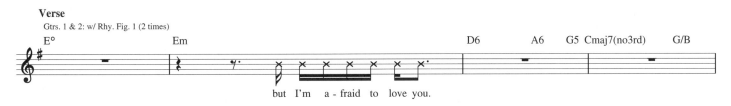

Whispered: I love you,   but I'm a-fraid to love you.   I'm a-fraid.   Oh, ____

⊕ Coda 2
Outro Chorus

Gsus2   Bm9

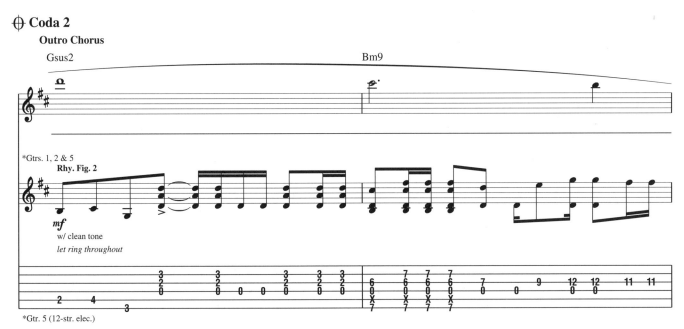

*Gtrs. 1, 2 & 5
Rhy. Fig. 2

mf
w/ clean tone
let ring throughout

*Gtr. 5 (12-str. elec.)

Vancouver

Words and Music by Jeff Buckley, Michael Tighe, Mick Grondahl and Matt Johnson

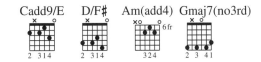

Gtrs. 1 & 3: Open D tuning:
(low to high) D–A–D–F#–A–D

Intro

*Gtr. 1
(12-str. elec.)

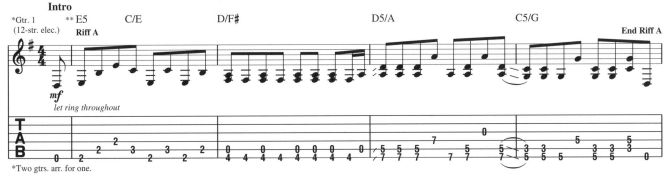

*Two gtrs. arr. for one.

**Chord symbols reflect implied harmony.

Gtr. 1: w/ Riff A

1. La -

Verse

Gtr. 1: w/ Riff A (3 3/4 times)

- dy,   oh,   the trem - ors of my ___ fright,   I ___ dis - gust ___

you. ___   I feel ___   the pow - er, you cut the truth ___ in two. ___

___   Why ___   do you think I'd hid - den out ___ on ___ this ___ lit - tle lie? ___

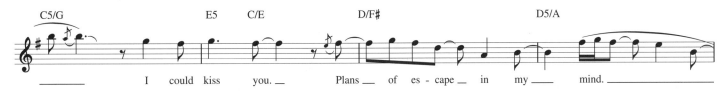

___   I could kiss you. ___ Plans ___ of es - cape ___ in my ___ mind. ___

Cadd9/E   D/F♯   D/F♯   Am(add4)   Gmaj7(no3rd)

did-n't leave at all. ___   You made an e-ven call. ___   My

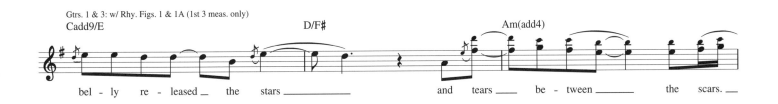

Gtrs. 1 & 3: w/ Rhy. Figs. 1 & 1A (1st 3 meas. only)

Cadd9/E   D/F♯   Am(add4)

bel-ly re-leased ___ the stars ___   and tears ___ be-tween ___ the scars. ___

Interlude

Gtr. 3 tacet

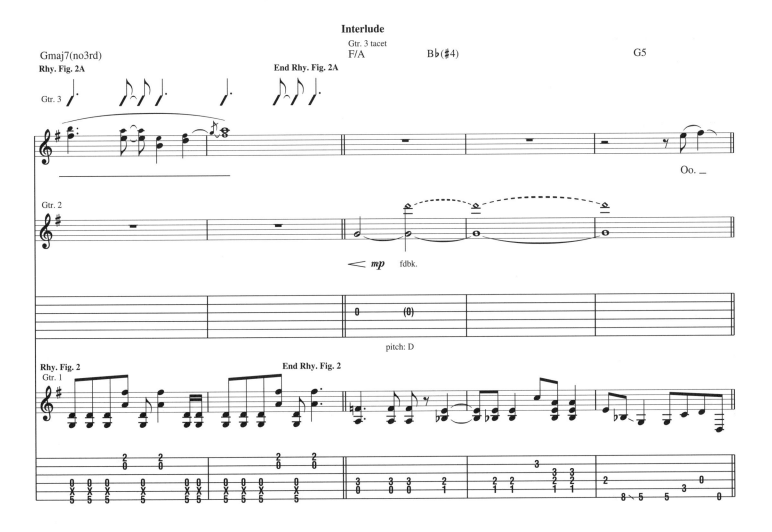

Gmaj7(no3rd)   F/A   B♭(♯4)   G5

Oo. ___

Gtr. 1: w/ Riff B

I am your failed ____ hus - band, con - tend - er. I'm your loan shark __ of __

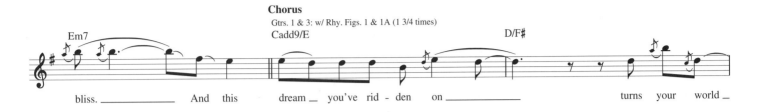

Chorus
Gtrs. 1 & 3: w/ Rhy. Figs. 1 & 1A (1 3/4 times)

bliss. _____ And this dream __ you've rid - den on ____ turns your world __

__ to ex - plo - sions. ____ I need to be a - lone ____

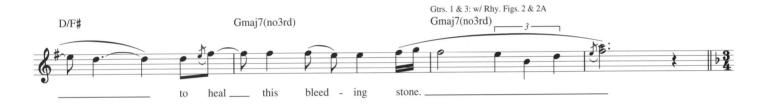

Gtrs. 1 & 3: w/ Rhy. Figs. 2 & 2A

_____ to heal __ this bleed - ing stone. ____

Bridge

Now _____ smell ____ the rain of __ Lon - don. __ It still __ in -

Gtr. 1

sists _____ that we beg ___ for _____ our,

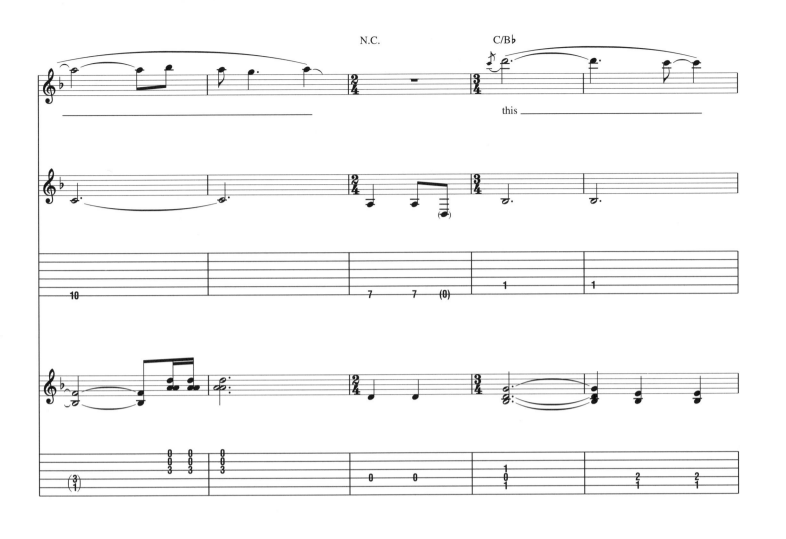

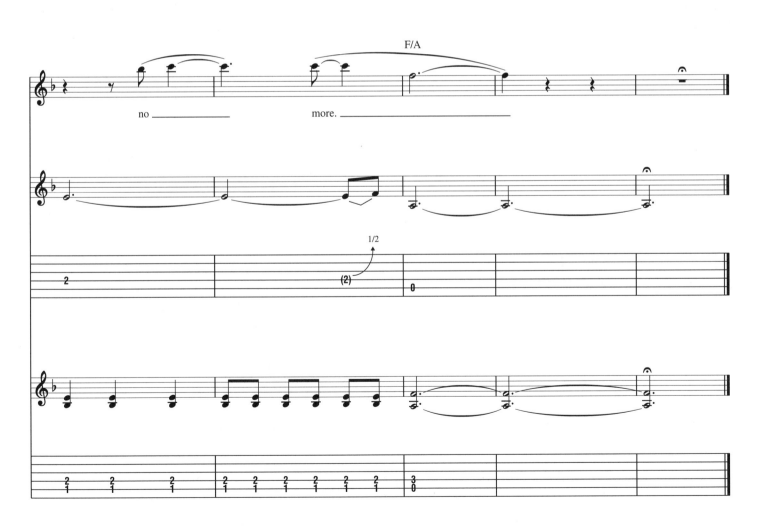

from *Mystery White Boy*

What Will You Say

Words and Music by Jeff Buckley, Chris Dowd and Carla Azar

Time feels like it's flown ___ a-way. ___
Fa - ther do you hear me? Do you know ___ me?

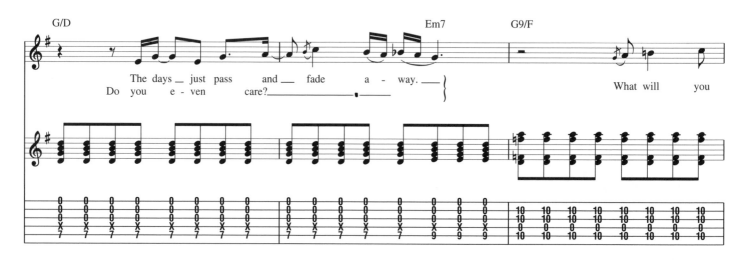

The days ___ just pass and ___ fade a - way. ___
Do you e - ven care? ___

What will you

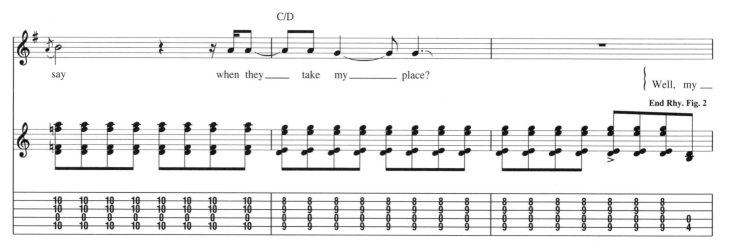

say when they ___ take my ___ place?

Well, my ___

* Gtr. 1: w/ Rhy. Fig. 2

Well, it's ___ fun-ny now. ___
___ heart

can't take this ___ an-y-more.
I just don't feel like I'm a man. ___

*Cresc., next 8 meas.

___
___
What will you ___ say
What will you say

when you ___ see my ___ face?
when you ___ see my ___ face?

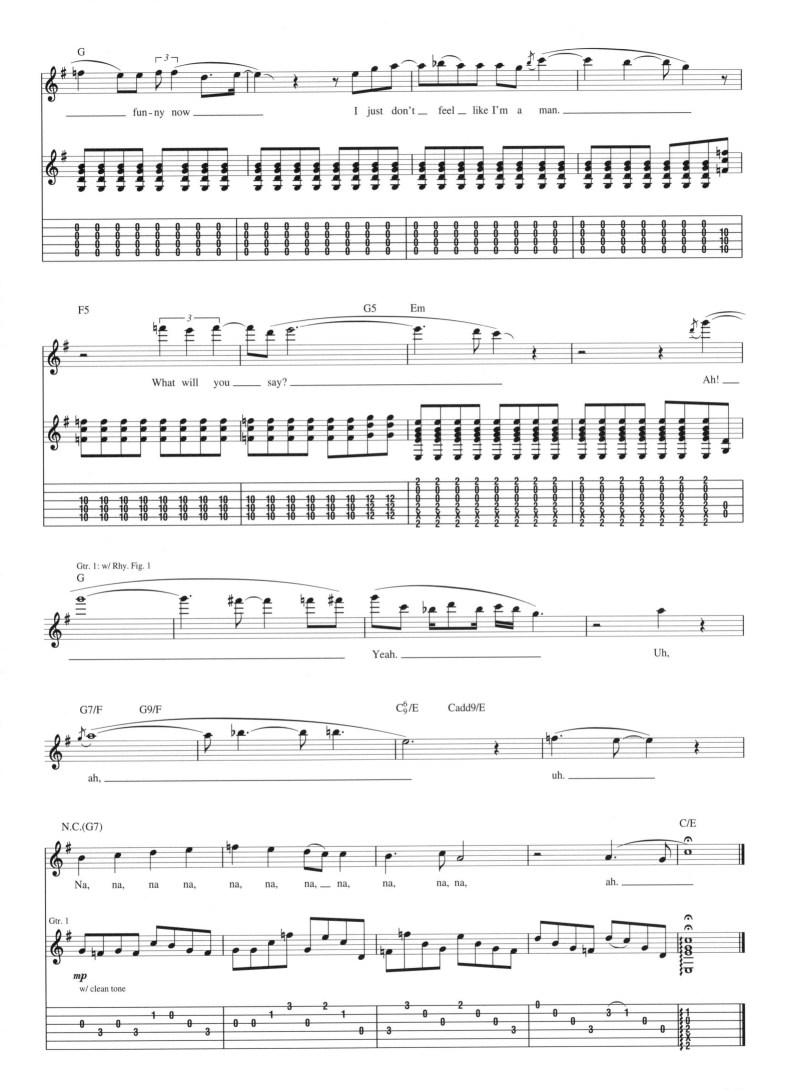

Witches' Rave

Words and Music by Jeff Buckley

*Chord symbols reflect combined harmony.

147

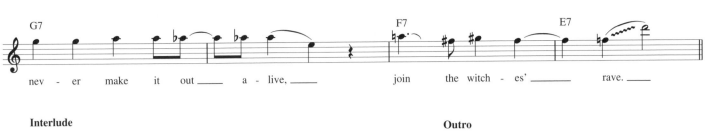

never make it out ___ a - live, ___ join the witch - es' ___ rave. ___

Interlude
Gtrs. 1 & 2: w/ Rhy. Figs. 1 & 1A (3 times)

Outro
Gtr. 3: w/ Riff B (2 times)

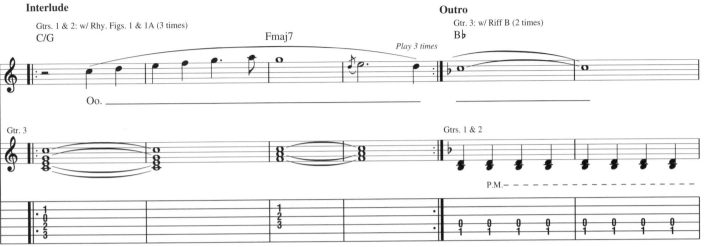

Oo. ___

Outro Chorus
Gtrs. 1 & 2: w/ Rhy. Fig. 3 (7 times)
Gtr. 3: w/ Riff B (14 times)

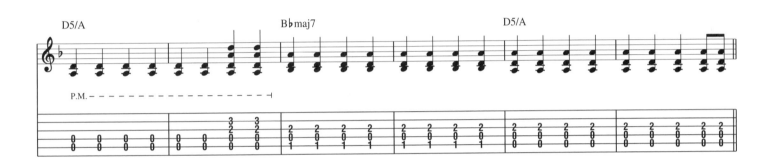

I can't help from look - ing ___ out - side ___ for a

guar - an - tee, ___ oh. ___

for a guar - an - tee. ___

Guitar Notation Legend

Guitar Music can be notated three different ways: on a *musical staff*, in *tablature*, and in *rhythm slashes*.

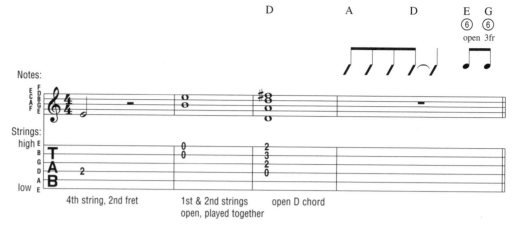

RHYTHM SLASHES are written above the staff. Strum chords in the rhythm indicated. Use the chord diagrams found at the top of the first page of the transcription for the appropriate chord voicings. Round noteheads indicate single notes.

THE MUSICAL STAFF shows pitches and rhythms and is divided by bar lines into measures. Pitches are named after the first seven letters of the alphabet.

TABLATURE graphically represents the guitar fingerboard. Each horizontal line represents a a string, and each number represents a fret.

4th string, 2nd fret

1st & 2nd strings open, played together

open D chord

Definitions for Special Guitar Notation

HALF-STEP BEND: Strike the note and bend up 1/2 step.

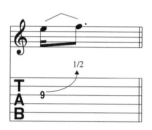

WHOLE-STEP BEND: Strike the note and bend up one step.

GRACE NOTE BEND: Strike the note and immediately bend up as indicated.

SLIGHT (MICROTONE) BEND: Strike the note and bend up 1/4 step.

BEND AND RELEASE: Strike the note and bend up as indicated, then release back to the original note. Only the first note is struck.

PRE-BEND: Bend the note as indicated, then strike it.

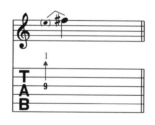

PRE-BEND AND RELEASE: Bend the note as indicated. Strike it and release the bend back to the original note.

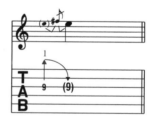

UNISON BEND: Strike the two notes simultaneously and bend the lower note up to the pitch of the higher.

VIBRATO: The string is vibrated by rapidly bending and releasing the note with the fretting hand.

WIDE VIBRATO: The pitch is varied to a greater degree by vibrating with the fretting hand.

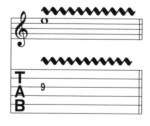

HAMMER-ON: Strike the first (lower) note with one finger, then sound the higher note (on the same string) with another finger by fretting it without picking.

PULL-OFF: Place both fingers on the notes to be sounded. Strike the first note and without picking, pull the finger off to sound the second (lower) note.

LEGATO SLIDE: Strike the first note and then slide the same fret-hand finger up or down to the second note. The second note is not struck.

SHIFT SLIDE: Same as legato slide, except the second note is struck.

TRILL: Very rapidly alternate between the notes indicated by continuously hammering on and pulling off.

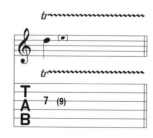

TAPPING: Hammer ("tap") the fret indicated with the pick-hand index or middle finger and pull off to the note fretted by the fret hand.

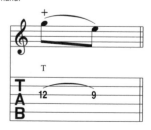

NATURAL HARMONIC: Strike the note while the fret-hand lightly touches the string directly over the fret indicated.

PINCH HARMONIC: The note is fretted normally and a harmonic is produced by adding the edge of the thumb or the tip of the index finger of the pick hand to the normal pick attack.

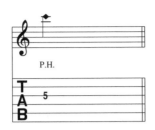

HARP HARMONIC: The note is fretted normally and a harmonic is produced by gently resting the pick hand's index finger directly above the indicated fret (in parentheses) while the pick hand's thumb or pick assists by plucking the appropriate string.

PICK SCRAPE: The edge of the pick is rubbed down (or up) the string, producing a scratchy sound.

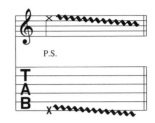

MUFFLED STRINGS: A percussive sound is produced by laying the fret hand across the string(s) without depressing, and striking them with the pick hand.

PALM MUTING: The note is partially muted by the pick hand lightly touching the string(s) just before the bridge.

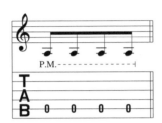

RAKE: Drag the pick across the strings indicated with a single motion.

TREMOLO PICKING: The note is picked as rapidly and continuously as possible.

ARPEGGIATE: Play the notes of the chord indicated by quickly rolling them from bottom to top.

VIBRATO BAR DIVE AND RETURN: The pitch of the note or chord is dropped a specified number of steps (in rhythm) then returned to the original pitch.

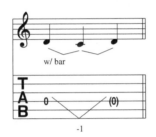

VIBRATO BAR SCOOP: Depress the bar just before striking the note, then quickly release the bar.

VIBRATO BAR DIP: Strike the note and then immediately drop a specified number of steps, then release back to the original pitch.

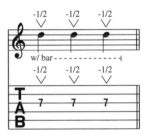

Additional Musical Definitions

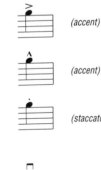

(accent)	• Accentuate note (play it louder)	
(accent)	• Accentuate note with great intensity	
(staccato)	• Play the note short	
⊓	• Downstroke	
V	• Upstroke	

D.S. al Coda • Go back to the sign (𝄋), then play until the measure marked "***To Coda***," then skip to the section labelled "**Coda**."

D.C. al Fine • Go back to the beginning of the song and play until the measure marked "***Fine***" (end).

Rhy. Fig. • Label used to recall a recurring accompaniment pattern (usually chordal).

Riff • Label used to recall composed, melodic lines (usually single notes) which recur.

Fill • Label used to identify a brief melodic figure which is to be inserted into the arrangement.

Rhy. Fill • A chordal version of a Fill.

tacet • Instrument is silent (drops out).

• Repeat measures between signs.

• When a repeated section has different endings, play the first ending only the first time and the second ending only the second time.

NOTE: Tablature numbers in parentheses mean:
1. The note is being sustained over a system (note in standard notation is tied), or
2. The note is sustained, but a new articulation (such as a hammer-on, pull-off, slide or vibrato begins), or
3. The note is a barely audible "ghost" note (note in standard notation is also in parentheses).

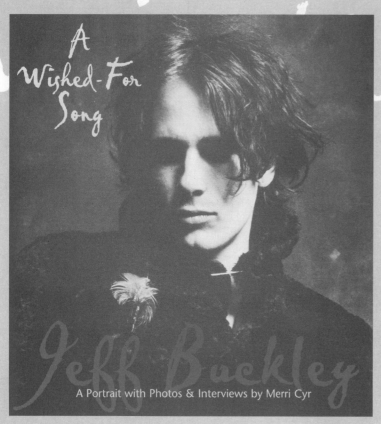